Princess Unaware

finding the *fabulous* in every day

brenda garrison

Standard®
PUBLISHING
Bringing The Word to Life

Cincinnati, Ohio

Published by Standard Publishing, Cincinnati, Ohio
www.standardpub.com

Substantive editor: Diane Stortz
Project editor: Lynn Lusby Pratt
Cover design: Brand Navigation
Interior design: Edward Willis Group, Inc.

ISBN 978-0-7847-2118-6

Library of Congress Cataloging-in-Publication Data

Garrison, Brenda, 1959-
Princess unaware : finding the fabulous in every day / Brenda Garrison.
  p. cm.
Includes bibliographical references.
ISBN 978-0-7847-2118-6
1. Christian women--Religious life. I. Title.

BV4527.G38 2009
248.8'43--dc22   2009008419

15 14 13 12 11 10 09   9 8 7 6 5 4 3 2 1

To my dear friend Myfanwy

The LORD your God is with you,
he is mighty to save.
He will take great delight in you,
he will quiet you with his love,
he will rejoice over you with singing.

—Zephaniah 3:17

Thanks and Praise

to God for allowing me to do the thing he put in me.
Thank you to my number-one cheerleader—my husband, Gene.
And thanks to our daughters, Katie, Kelsey, and Kerry,
who think it is so cool that their mom writes books and who
patiently help me with the techie stuff that I am forever learning.
Thank you to Lena Wood for working her magic on the fairy tale.

Special thanks to the fabulous people at Standard Publishing
who believe in me. They have become dear friends,
and I appreciate them all so much.

One more thank-you to Eric, Deb, Danielle, and Teri.

Contents

A Note from Brenda

I am thrilled to have you on this journey with me. I pray the biblical truths here will transform your life and relationship with God as they have transformed mine and continue to do so.

Princess Unaware consists of ten chapters, each containing a four-day study at the end. I hope you won't just go through the material—I want the material to go through you! There are several ways this can be accomplished. I will suggest a couple.

For Individual Study

I recommend doing a chapter per week. Take three days to read the chapter and then do the study over the next four days. This way the principles have time to be absorbed into your thoughts as you work through the chapter and go about your week.

For Small Group Study

Princess Unaware would make an excellent ten-week course for your Bible study group. As with the suggestion for individual study, your group members would read the chapter and do the four-day study on their own during the week—and then discuss everything when you meet together. Or the group could read the chapter during your time together, briefly discuss it, and then encourage members to do the study on their own at home.

Choose or create a plan that works best for you or your group. You'll also be prompted throughout the book to write in or refer to the Royal Truths, a section where you will personalize key points. Even after you've finished the book, you'll be able to return to these pages as a mini refresher course.

Enjoy the journey—from living as Princess Unaware to finding the fabulous in every day!

chapter one

Crawling Out of the Mud Hole

The Princess Recognizes the Traps and Snares

I hate icebreaker games, wedding shower games, and baby shower games. One game I especially don't like is the describe-yourself-in-three-words game. I resent the insinuation that I can be summed up in three words. You too are a deep and complicated person, so three words will hardly help us really get to know each other. However, if I had to choose three words to describe myself, I would choose *enthusiastic, inquisitive,* and *passionate.*

Did I win the prize? *Enthusiastic. Inquisitive. Passionate.* These words drive me to live my life with purpose. Knowing that these words describe me will help you understand why I wrote this book and why I am excited that *you* are reading it!

Enthusiastic. I get excited about doing life well and the fabulous things that happen along the way, whether talking with another woman for five minutes and feeling like we've known each other for years, or celebrating with a dear friend who has achieved her dream after years of preparation and work.

Inquisitive. I want to know the source of information. (It's not that I don't trust you; I just need to know how you know.) I ask questions. *How can I make a difference? What was I made to do? How can I enjoy life? How can I do life so as not to have all this guilt and frustration?*

Passionate. What excites me in life, I am passionate about. Why spend time and emotion and energy on something if I'm not passionate about it?

Since we started the game, let's finish it. What three words would you use to describe yourself? How do those adjectives reflect the way you live? Are those words getting you to a place of fulfillment, or is something missing? If the adjectives you used are full of despair, guilt, and fear . . . or apathy, carelessness, and passiveness, I want to ignite your life with the truth and hope befitting a princess, because if you know Jesus, you're a child of the King! And if you don't know Jesus (or even *about* Jesus), keep reading and I'll introduce you.

For much of my life, I was on a quest for something to make my enthusiasm count, to answer my questions, to be worthy of my passion. I kept hearing I was a princess of the King, but I couldn't find my crown, much less keep it on my head. I searched in places that appeared to have what I was looking for—relationships, church, Bible studies, ministry, at-home businesses, doing all the right things. Somehow I kept missing it—the *umph*, the *fabulous* that I knew would be worthy of my enthusiasm, inquisitiveness, and passion.

But I did eventually find answers to my questions. God brought to me his truth that was so applicable. His answers made sense, and they made sense together. Throughout this book, I'll share with you the answers I found and how I know they are true and right. But first let's read about another young woman on a journey for answers. She's a lot like I was. She might be like you today.

The Journey of a Princess Unaware

The time had come. Jess's packed satchel sat by the front door. She came from her room, dressed for the big expedition.

"Mother, I'm ready."

"I hope so," Mother murmured, swallowing hard to hold back tears.

"What?" Jess asked, fingering the jeweled gold crest she wore around her neck. It was almost a part of her; she couldn't remember ever not wearing it.

"I know you're ready," Mother answered tentatively. But her eyes revealed doubt.

Mother and Father had been preparing Jess for this moment since she was a small child. Jess had known her time with Mother and Father was limited and that when she turned eighteen, they must send her to the castle in the Faraway Land.

"Mother, now that I am leaving, I must ask you . . . why have you and Father always called me Princess?"

"You will find out soon enough, dear."

"But where is the castle, and how do I get there?"

"Princess," Father said as he joined them, "remember the signs I taught you. Follow Polaris north until you see the mountains. Then turn west until you reach the Forest of Amusements. Go around it and continue west. Beware of Pit Weasels, of Glittering Greens and Scaly Reds," he warned.

Jess gasped. "What are those?!"

"You must see them for yourself," he said simply.

Her mother nodded, biting her lip worriedly.

"And take this," Father said as he handed her a well-worn book.

"But Father, this is the book you have taught me from since I was a little girl. I can't understand it without you."

"Yes, you can. I have taught you everything I know from the book, and you have learned well. Use what you have learned on your journey." Father put the book into the side pocket of Jess's satchel, turning away to hide his damp eyes.

"But how far is it? How will I know if I get off course? Will anyone at the castle be expecting me? What will I do there?" Jess had always trusted Mother and Father about the big expedition, but now she needed answers.

"I'm sorry. I've told you all I can. Now it's time for you to leave," urged her father.

Jess hugged and kissed Mother and Father, picked up her satchel, and walked out of the house and down the lane. She turned and headed north, resolving not to let anything stop her from arriving at her destination.

Her day was uneventful. The sky was blue, the breeze gentle, the forest calm and dark. She found herself saying out loud, "Why, this journey is not difficult at all! What a pleasant stroll I will have to the castle in the Faraway Land."

Scarcely had she spoken when . . . she rounded a bend and spotted a pack of strange creatures in the road. They were small and dark, furry, bustling things—with huge heads, long thin tails, and sharp little teeth and claws. Some were digging in the road; others were dragging brush from the forest with their teeth, scattering it over the holes, and covering the holes with dry grass and dirt.

They're setting a trap for travelers, she realized, *to trip them unawares and leave them to die . . . or worse, to devour them!*

"Pit Weasels!" she cried. The creatures stopped in unison, stood on their hind legs, and looked at her, their eyes gleaming maliciously.

"Go away!" she yelled. She swung her satchel in wide circles, as if she were going to hurl it at them. "Get out of my way!"

They darted into the dark forest. Jess hurried past, keeping her eyes on the path.

That night she camped under a grove of evergreens. Before the fire went out, she tried to read some of the book Father gave her. *Maybe this will help take my mind off those dreadful Pit Weasels,* she told herself. Much of what she read didn't make sense. *I knew I needed Father to help me understand this,* she thought. But as she read on, a peace and comfort covered her like a warm blanket. She rested her head on the book and fell asleep.

When a gorgeous new day dawned, Jess awoke and looked forward to making significant progress in her travels. She remembered the evil forest creatures. Her fear was quickly chased away by her resolve not to be trapped by them.

Late in the morning, dark clouds moved in, and suddenly Jess found herself in a downpour. She ran under a rocky ledge for shelter. As the rain let up, she decided to continue on. "If I let every raindrop stop me, I will never get to the castle," she reasoned.

The terrain turned rocky and gradually steepened. She didn't see the slippery rock her foot landed on, and down she went.

"Ick! My dress is soaked . . . and muddy." She stood up and pushed her wet hair out of her face. "Ugh. My hands are muddy too. I'm a mess."

There was no stream to wash in, but Jess did her best to get most of the mud off. "I'm not letting a little mud slow me down," she said, continuing on her journey. "Father told me to get there, no matter what."

Jess made great progress. Toward twilight she came upon a green meadow with a little brook in the distance. "Fresh water!" she exclaimed. "What a lovely place to camp!" Excitedly she ran toward the brook . . . and right into a very deep hole in the path, one that had been camouflaged with underbrush and a thin layer of dirt and grass.

Struggling out of the hole, she heard skittering and snickering. From the dark cover of the forest, many pairs of eyes gleamed at her. Pit Weasels! Terrified, she cried out, "Oh, Father!" She searched frantically for her satchel. "Oh, what shall I do!" She had no other weapon. How she wished for her father!

Out skittered the Pit Weasels, snickering as they scurried toward her. Suddenly, they looked toward the sky, stopped, and ran squealing back into the underbrush.

What? Jess followed their gaze . . . High overhead a lone falcon circled. Greatly relieved, she climbed out of the hole, thankful for the raptor's presence.

Do you ever feel like Jess—not ready for what life brings, slipping into mess after mess, falling for traps others set for you? Jess has much going for her. She was raised well, she has the book of wisdom from which her father taught her, and an exciting future waits for her. However, despite these benefits, she is not doing well on her journey.

Maybe you feel you don't have any of Jess's assets. Maybe you didn't have a loving, caring family. Maybe you have never been taught wisdom or life skills. Maybe you were told you'd never amount to much, so you don't expect much. If any of this is true, my heart aches for you, and at the same time, I'm thrilled for you! Because no matter where you have come from or what lies you were told, you are loved and cared for by your Father in Heaven. "'I know the plans I have for you,' declares the LORD, 'plans to prosper you and not to harm you, plans to give you hope and a future'" (Jeremiah 29:11).

Or maybe, like Jess, you have much going for you—but you still aren't living a rich life. You feel stuck. You are ricocheting through life, hoping that someday you will stop and make changes to really live to the fullest. But someday hasn't come.

Now is the time. Let's journey with Jess and learn the truths that will make a difference. We'll apply those truths to our everyday lives together. Living in the reality of truth is what enables us to find the fabulous in every day. That is a promise our Savior gave us: "The thief comes only in order to steal and kill and destroy. I came that they may have and enjoy life, and have it in abundance (to the full, till it overflows)" (John 10:10, *AMP*).

Why We Stumble

I believe women stumble into several common mud holes and traps. Since we are relational, we often follow each other into the messes. But if we know the truth about who we are, whose we are, who God is, and the rich life God has for us, we will be prepared to avoid these traps. Our lives don't have to be one regret or frustration after another!

Who Are You?

The first reason we fall into mud holes and traps is that we don't know who we are. We don't value ourselves as made in the image of our Father. We believe our worth depends on the checkbook balance, our careers, parenting success, or a Pilates-sculpted body. Throughout our lives we have absorbed lies about ourselves—that we are untalented, unintelligent, irritating, unattractive, too skinny, too fat, unpopular, and ultimately unworthy.

Maybe you've made poor choices that contributed to the list of lies you now believe, so because of your past *and* present, you feel like a failure and the worst of sinners. And because your past is fact, it must be the truth of who you are. Right? Wrong. Remember Jeremiah 29:11 used words like *plans, prosper,* and *hope.* That verse is full of promise for the future. We are not victims of our past, whether we chose it or not. Our Lord has plans for us. Our part is to get on track with him and get going in his direction.

Another important factor contributing to knowing who we are is the insecurity we battle. I have never met an adult woman who doesn't struggle with insecurity on some level. Our insecurities take control of our intelligent minds and convince us to believe lies about ourselves, which in turn affect our decisions and actions. We see the results of this in our relationships. We worry about what other women are thinking about us.

- ✦ *Did I say the wrong thing?*
- ✦ *Did I wear the wrong thing?*
- ✦ *Why didn't I get invited?*
- ✦ *Did I handle that well?*
- ✦ *Did I offend her?*

Our insecurities and poor self-image cause us to falter. To fit in and be accepted, we try to be someone we are not. Self-doubt consumes us. Under the influence of our insecurities, we do and say things that might have been expected when we were younger. A young wife once shared with me how she enjoyed meeting with her girlfriends from high school for an evening of Bunco . . . until their conversation quickly turned into a discussion she knew she shouldn't be part of.

We all enjoy friends—it's the way God wired us. Nothing hurts more than to be left out or ignored. We assume we are the problem, and we doubt our value as a person and friend. Please don't wallow any longer in the lies whispered by insecurity. Keep reading, and you will see how loved you are.

Whose Are You?

The next reason we stumble into mud holes and traps is that we don't know *whose* we are. You are here on earth by God's divine and perfect plan. Not believing that truth leaves a long blank space in the description of who you are. Not knowing that the one and only, holy, Almighty God created you and designed you for a specific plan leaves you without direction and purpose.

If you believe you are here because a froglike creature crawled out of the water onto land that was produced by a big bang in the sky (even though no one knows where the necessary elements to cause the bang came from) and that the froglike creature evolved into a monkey and the monkey evolved into your ancestors and you were born at random—then no wonder you are floundering and lacking self-worth! We are not the result of millions of years of random science experiments. We have a loving heavenly Father who created us: "You created my inmost being; you knit me together in my mother's womb" (Psalm 139:13). I will talk more about this in chapters 2 and 3, but know that you are not an accident. God was looking forward to your birth.

Who Is God?

The next reason we fall is that we don't know God. Most likely you have absorbed lies about God all your life. Even well intended half-truths can lead us astray. The secular world certainly has its interpretation of God, Jesus, Heaven, angels, and all things spiritual. Take a look in any national chain bookstore at the number of shelves provided for the "spirituality" and "religion" titles. The world is getting the attention of people who are curious about spiritual matters but who distrust the church.

Even in churches we may have been taught or absorbed information about God that is not true. It may have been presented as truth by teachers and preachers who believed it to be true, but have we checked out for ourselves what they were teaching?

Hey, they're the experts, right? But if we've learned about God through what others have told us, not by firsthand study and experience, isn't that what the secular world is doing? I am not saying we can't trust our pastors and Bible teachers. I respect and honor the men and women who have taught me God's Word and how to apply it to my life. But it's OK to question them. We must compare what we are taught to the Word of God to ensure the accuracy of the teaching. Paul praised the believers in Berea for doing this: "The Bereans . . . received the message with great eagerness and examined the Scriptures every day to see if what Paul said was true" (Acts 17:11).

Suppose a writer wanted to write a book about you. This writer interviewed every person who knew you or interacted with you or just knew about you. He gathered their "facts" about you but never talked to you. Then he wrote his book. Would you trust his version of you? I wouldn't. I know people don't see me the way I really am. Some see me better, some worse. I wouldn't want to be judged wholly by what others said about me.

Yet that is what we do to God when we think we know him but have only listened to what others tell us about him. Their versions of God are colored by their views and life experiences. If we are going to get to know God, we need to get into the truth about himself that he has given us—the Bible. We need to establish and develop a relationship with him. Then we can know if what we are hearing about God is true.

Satan Wants You to Miss God's Plan

When we don't know who we are, whose we are, and who God is, we miss the rich life God has for us. We settle for status quo because that's all we (or anyone else) expect from ourselves. Like the shiny-eyed creatures in Jess's story, lurking in the dark perimeters, our enemy sets many traps for us and snickers when he gets us. Yes, you have an enemy if you are a child of God (see 1 Peter 5:8)! Our enemy will use whatever tools are most effective on each individual person.

Discouragement

Discouragement is one of Satan's favorite and effective tools. He knows it is often easier to disable us with discouragement than to sideline us because of sin. If we are living with a sinful habit, we develop a sense of denial inflated by pride;

pride keeps us thinking we are doing great and that God is lucky to have us working for him. When we are discouraged, however, we believe ridiculous lies about ourselves, we remove God from the equation, and we head for the bench with our heads down. We wonder why God thought it was a good idea to get us involved in his kingdom work. As we slump on the bench, the enemy whispers his famous line: "Did God really say . . . ?" (Genesis 3:1), and we drown in doubt—did we ever really hear from God? We question whether God meant our job, ministry, family, or dream for someone else whose conversation we overheard.

No way! God's good plan for you *is for you*. I know how tempting discouragement is. I know what it feels like to think I'm unequipped for the task God puts on my to-do list. From parenting (my book *Queen Mom* tells the story) to writing books (who me?—a stay-at-home mom in the cornfields of Illinois?) to any number of ministry opportunities God has assigned to me, I have not felt like the best person for the job. But God loves using people who don't feel as if they have it all together. Read through the New Testament and savor the way Jesus picked, transformed, and then used regular guys to spread the gospel throughout the world. Discouragement is a mud hole that sucks you down, disables you, and keeps you from your rich life.

Fear

The next effective trap is fear, the most addressed issue in the Bible! Fear keeps us stuck, paralyzed, afraid to move on or even to move sideways. *Why, who knows* what *will happen if I:*

+ *take the class, job, or promotion?*
+ *move to a new city?*
+ *marry the guy who seems to be Mr. Right?*
+ *start a family even though I don't feel prepared?*
+ *try to make friends?*
+ *do that thing God has been talking to me about for the longest time?*

Fear keeps us from the life God planned for us. While I lunched with a group of women, one of them said, "I had a book contract once."

"Ooh, really!" I was excited to hear about her adventure.

"Yes, but I got part way into it and then I couldn't go on."

"But why?"

"I just couldn't. I froze."

My heart broke for her. She had come so far! Her goal to be published had been within her grasp. Then fear grabbed her, and she couldn't move. Fear stole her dream. She has gone on with her life and does other ministry well, but my heart still aches for the dream the enemy snatched while she was under his spell of fear.

Do You Want to Get Well?

The enemy has other traps that are effective and socially acceptable, even in Christian circles. Many women use the poor-me syndrome so they can stay stuck. But this is just laziness and excuse making in disguise. When we surrender to the poor-me syndrome, other Christians are obliged to show mercy and grace. If they didn't, what kind of Christians would they be? Who would dare challenge us with the truth of the Word that would get us out of our comfy mud holes?

Hmm, I'm thinking maybe Jesus.

In John 5:1-9, we see Jesus at the pool of water near the Sheep Gate in Jerusalem. Many disabled people lay there because "from time to time an angel of the Lord would come down and stir up the waters. The first one into the pool after each such disturbance would be cured of whatever disease he had" (v. 4). Jesus walked up to one man and asked him, "Do you want to get well?" (v. 6). The man gave him an excuse. Then Jesus got to the root of the issue: "Get up! Pick up your mat and walk." The story concludes, "At once the man was cured; he picked up his mat and walked" (vv. 8, 9).

Dear Princess Unaware, I must ask you the same question: Do you want to get well? Do you want to get up out of your mess of laziness and excuses and move on with the exciting life God has for you? Are you willing to do as this man did and act on your desire, to "pick up your mat and walk"?

Perfectionism and Procrastination

These last two traps can also be disguised acceptably in Christian circles.

Perfectionism is not the same as wanting to do our best. I am all for doing what we do with excellence. No, perfectionism is another form of paralyzing fear. Perfectionism demands that everything be perfect. The problem with perfectionism is that nothing we do will ever be perfect enough; therefore, we do nothing. We are so stuck in the paralyzing fear—believing our efforts won't be good enough—that we can't go on. Pretty effective trap.

Procrastination works as well as perfectionism. In today's fast-paced society, busyness is a status symbol. The excuses "I didn't have time" or "I'll get to it when I can" are accepted with graciousness and empathy. So when God lays an opportunity in our laps, we gently take it and put it to the side to do when we get time. And of course, we never do get time. We stay stuck in the mud hole of procrastination. We don't proceed, and we don't accomplish what God planned for us to do for the kingdom. The enemy snickers.

Princess Training

Before you start to think the purpose of this book is to help you feel good and be your best self, it is not. I took you through that spiritual noodle lashing to help you see that life isn't all about us. It's all about God—knowing him, having a relationship with him, and glorifying him by living the life he planned for us.

Have you thought about how the junk in your life keeps you from the real life God planned for you? Princess Unaware, we need to get a clue here, to get our eyes and ears tuned in to God to discover who he is, who we are, what he has for us—and then get at it. And while God's deepest desire is for us all to be his princesses, the truth is, it is our choice to become princesses or to remain peasants. (More about this in chapter 2!) This life on earth won't last forever. We can't afford to waste any of it.

Now it's your turn.

The study section at the end of every chapter, Finding the Fabulous, will lead you to sit at the Lord's feet and hear from him yourself—to help you talk to him and let him talk to you, directing, guiding, and changing you. In getting to know

God through reading and studying the Word, and thinking about how to apply it, we can make changes in our lives. We'll be challenged to examine the beliefs we have been operating on until now.

Included in Day One will be Looking Ahead, a short section to help focus on what we will learn and how you might incorporate it into your life. And on Day Four we'll take time for Looking Back on how we did during the week.

You can complete the Finding the Fabulous pages on your own or share in this study with your small group.

Finding the Fabulous

Looking Ahead

How would you rate the richness of your life—your worth as a child of the King? your relationships with God, family, friends? your purpose and direction in life? Do you feel stuck in any area of life?

✦ ✦ ✦ ✦ ✦ ✦ ✦ ✦ ✦ ✦ ✦

DAY ONE: Self-Help Is No Help

The self-help mentality is everywhere. Much of the time self-help delivers a pseudo-Christian message. When have you been tempted to go to the secular gospel for answers and direction?

What part of the world's teaching have you believed and even incorporated into your life?

In our Princess Unaware story, Jess realized early in her adventure that she was not prepared for the mud holes she came upon or the traps of the Pit Weasels. What about you? What messy issues do you need to deal with?

Until now have you believed that you have an enemy who wants to keep you from the rich life Christ has for you? Why or why not?

Read 1 Peter 5:8. What mental picture do you get?

This is fact, not an analogy: our enemy is looking to get us. We need to be ready. Now let's look at Matthew 13:24-30, 36-39. In this parable Jesus shows us that an enemy actively works to counteract God's plan. When have you experienced trying to do better, to help someone, or to do a project for God but felt that you were getting nowhere?

One more nugget for you—read Ephesians 6:10-18. The study of this Scripture could be a book on its own, but let's look at verses 12, 13. Who is our enemy?

What is our battle plan? (vv. 13-18).

God is *for* us. He has not left us without a plan. We need to be ready with the tools he has given us: the truth (we are discussing some of that in this book); the righteousness we have because of Jesus; the gospel; our faith, which deflects Satan's attack; our salvation, which keeps us secure in God; the Word of God; and finally, prayer. When you think of your future, what comes to mind? Are you excited? depressed? not expecting much—just the status quo?

Read Jeremiah 29:11. Now read it again, knowing that God is speaking to you. What does this verse say that God plans for you?

If you really believed Jeremiah 29:11, how would it change the way you think about your future?

God is promising to prosper you—personally—who you are—with the richness and abundance of life mentioned in John 10:10. What do you think that might look like for you?

Princess Unaware, our futures are gripped by God's hands. He loves us, wants what is best for us, and will work everything that comes into our lives for our benefit. "We know that God causes everything to work together for the good of those who love God and are called according to his purpose for them" (Romans 8:28, *NLT*).

Think About It

How do you feel knowing that your life is not a random event but that God has a plan specifically for you?

John 10:10 is the core inspiration for our journey together. I love the way the *Amplified Bible* states it: "The thief comes only in order to steal and kill and destroy. I came that they may have and enjoy life, and have it in abundance (to the full, till it overflows)." Ah, once again we see that we have an enemy whose goal is to harm us, even destroy us. But we have Jesus, who came not only to give us eternal life in Heaven but an abundant, rich life on earth. What do you think of as an abundant, rich life?

In Greek the word *abundance* in this verse means "superabundant (in quantity) or superior (in quality)," "excessive," "exceeding abundantly above," and "beyond measure."[1] The word *life* here means "vitality" and "lifetime."[2] When we put the two together, we have vitality of life beyond measure, superior in quality—a richness that can come only from God. This is not a promise of riches, comfort, ease, good health, or worldly success. But it *is* a promise that if we have Christ, our lives will have eternal meaning, depth, satisfaction, and fulfillment beyond what our finite minds can imagine. If you had to choose, which would you rather have—riches, ease, and success, or a life of eternal meaning, depth, and satisfaction? What's the attraction?

The truth is that the world may promise riches and success, but it can't deliver. However, Jesus promises us abundant, rich life, and he can and does deliver. I'm going with Jesus.

✦ ✦ ✦ ✦ ✦ ✦ ✦ ✦ ✦ ✦ ✦

DAY TWO: Lies, Lies, and More Lies

It's time to identify some of the mud holes we have been wallowing in for a while, maybe for years. We can get many negative messages from every area of our lives—family, friends, educators, the media, culture, and sometimes even from the church.

Identify the negative messages and lies about yourself that you have taken in as truth. I listed several examples in the chapter. (Please don't wallow in this and open past wounds. If you have healed and moved on, great! This exercise is not for you.)

If you have a past sin that you allow the enemy to beat you up with, confess it to God. "If we confess our sins, he is faithful and just and will forgive us our sins and purify us from all unrighteousness" (1 John 1:9). The sin is gone, and we can no longer let it hold us down. "There is now no condemnation for those who are in Christ Jesus" (Romans 8:1). Did you confess your sin to God? Good. Then it is history. It is neither your present nor your future. Remember Jeremiah 29:11—you have been promised hope and a future.

You are precious to God, and every part of you and your personality was designed by him. Read Psalm 139:1-16. Now read it again—taking it in as God speaking it to your heart, because he is. How do you feel, knowing you have this much attention from the Creator of the universe?

What do you think about yourself now that you know you are God's unique design—made just the way he wants you to be?

Knowing that God is with you every day and wants the best, what's one thing you could do today to bring your agenda in line with his plan for you?

Where have you gotten the majority of your information about God—from clergy, parents, books (secular or Christian), friends, people in your church, media personalities (secular or Christian), the Bible? List the main sources. Be honest.

How often do you check in the Bible to see if what you are hearing is true?

By spending time with people, we not only learn about them but also build relationship with them—we interact around a variety of issues. We begin to understand how they think and why they think the way they do. We observe how they handle situations. They pour into our lives and we pour into theirs. By spending time with God—letting him into our lives, reading the Bible, and talking with him—we get to know God personally.

Think About It

How would you feel if someone formed an opinion about you based only on what others said, and never bothered to talk to you personally? Has this ever happened to you?

From what we have learned about God so far, have you identified any lies or misconceptions about God that you have believed? List those here.

Think of a time you felt left out, snubbed, or devalued by a friend. Again, you are not allowed to beat yourself up; just give the facts.

Recently I fell for this trap of the enemy's. I assumed friends were doing something together and I was not invited. I stewed over it for half a day. The fact is that sometimes these friends do activities together without inviting me. I don't know why they do, but I came to realize that it is not my issue. Taking these things personally only makes me miserable and insecure. I am the best friend I know how to be; that will have to be enough. The final fact in this situation—I later learned they did *not* get together for the event. I made a wrong assumption. Oops!

Let's think about God's plan for our lives one more time. Sure, God wants what is best for us in this earthly life, but is there more than just status quo—getting a degree, going to work, raising a family, retiring? There is nothing wrong with any of those things. They are good things, but the key here is God's plan for us in all of it. Without God we are just going through these seasons of life.

Do you feel like you travel through life on a conveyer belt—going from one thing to the next with no time to savor the moment or enjoy experiences? How have you observed this in your life in the past year?

Think About It

Are you ready to sit at the Lord's feet and hear what he has for you? List the changes you will make to be in a mind-set to hear from God.

✦ ✦ ✦ ✦ ✦ ✦ ✦ ✦ ✦ ✦ ✦

DAY THREE: The Enemy's Most Effective Traps

The enemy's goal is to keep us from doing what God put us here to do.

Discouragement is sneaky. It seems benign while we are wallowing in it, but nothing renders us useless faster than discouragement. The last time you were discouraged, what were the circumstances?

As you listed your circumstances above, did you include the presence and power of God in your life? Read Habakkuk 3:17, 18 and then respond.

Think back. Did you ever hear Satan ever so subtly put this thought in your mind: *Did God really say . . .*

- ✦ *he will be with you even if you don't marry?*
- ✦ *he will take care of your financial needs?*
- ✦ *your life will be full even if you don't have children?*
- ✦ *you will be a good mom?*
- ✦ *to follow him by faith to do the task he is pressing on your heart?*
- ✦ *to do business by his book, the Bible?*

I know some of those questions might have stung a bit, and I'm sorry. But we must know that God is compassionate and attentive regarding the tender issues in our lives. "He heals the brokenhearted and binds up their wounds" (Psalm 147:3). I can't possibly cover all that God has promised us, but let's get a good start. What does God say in Hebrews 13:5, 6 (about money and his presence)?

Matthew 6:25-34 (about all of your physical needs)?

John 10:10 (about the richness of your life)?

Isaiah 52:12 (about his presence in your life and ministry)?

Philippians 4:13 (about how he'll equip you for whatever he puts on your to-do list)?

Psalm 138:8 (about all he has planned for you)?

How can you apply any of these truths to the tender issues in your life?

The above verses are only a smidgen of the truth God has for you in his Word. I encourage you to write down any verses that God speaks to you through. Carry them with you and meditate on those verses and what God wants to teach you. I buy index cards held together with rings. Then I can carry them anywhere I go—in my purse, on my walk, even around the house.

Fear is kindred to discouragement; fear also sneaks in and looks benign. We tend to equate fear with wisdom and caution, but it's not the same. Let's call it what it is—leaving God out of the equation. Fear factors out God. I find I am more fearful of the unknown than of what I know is coming at me. I may dread a difficult situation coming my way, but I can prepare for it with the Lord. I feel fear overcoming me when I am faced with a situation out of my frame of reference or experience. I have felt the suffocation of fear come over me when:

+ I have accepted new-to-me ministry opportunities.
+ I have traveled alone.

- I took on a project totally out of my realm of talent or giftedness because I knew it was a mission from God.
- I get near anything involving technology that I have not yet learned.
- I started doing radio and TV interviews. (Hint: When doing a TV interview, never cross the leg facing the camera. It will look like a huge ham—not flattering!)

The cool thing is that God took me through each fearful event, and many times my fear was extinguished before I came to the situation. You may look at my list of fears and think, *What a weenie!* So what is your list of fears?

The key to handling fear isn't to not feel fear; it's what we do with fear and how quickly we deal with it. The Bible is full of stories of people who were fearful in new or difficult situations. Read these accounts; then briefly identify the cause of fear in each one:

Exodus 3:1-14; 4:1, 10-17

Judges 6:11-40

Luke 1:26-38

The strong, confident princess knows she will have fear throughout her life, and she prepares herself to deal with it by trusting God and factoring him into all her circumstances.

✦ ✦ ✦ ✦ ✦ ✦ ✦ ✦ ✦ ✦ ✦

DAY FOUR: Mud Holes We Love to Wallow In

"Move over. I'm coming in!" We find lots of company in the mud holes we'll look at today. Not only are they easy to fall into; they are often considered acceptable. Most people won't challenge us to get out—they might even jump in and wallow with us.

The first mud hole is a mucky combination of laziness and excuse making. We can easily use these disguises to play down any hint of responsibility on our part, giving in to the poor-me syndrome. How do you define the poor-me syndrome?

Give an example of how you (*gasp*—of course not *you*, but a hypothetical you) might get stuck in this mud hole.

In what situations do you not only *fall* into the mud holes of laziness or excuse making but also intentionally visit them with your sunglasses and towel for a relaxing afternoon? I'm not talking about well-deserved time off to read, sit by the pool, or talk on the phone with a friend who lives miles away. I'm talking about the frequent temptation to waste time, to do nothing when responsibilities wait, or to make excuses to yourself and others for your behavior.

You are a princess! Get out of that muck! "Never be lazy, but work hard and serve the Lord enthusiastically" (Romans 12:11, *NLT*). How does this verse challenge or encourage you?

Proverbs 26:13 says, "The lazy person claims, 'There's a lion on the road! Yes, I'm sure there's a lion out there!'" (*NLT*). Have you found yourself making these excuses for your laziness?

+ "When we get more money, I will get the house in order."

- ✦ "When the kids are gone, I will get myself in order."
- ✦ "When things settle down, I will get my relationship with the Lord in order."

What is an excuse you use to delay doing the next thing God has shown you?

Some of the excuses we use could be the result of believing the lies of the enemy. For example, there are excuses that fall under the category of "I could never do that":

- ✦ "I'm not talented enough."
- ✦ "I'm not good with people."
- ✦ "I'm not smart enough."
- ✦ "I'm not disciplined enough."
- ✦ "I don't have the time."

What handy excuses do you recite to the Lord when he presents you with an adventure? Be bold. List them here.

 ## One More Thing

I know I'm being brutal here, but it is because I love you and want God's best for you. Reread John 5:1-9. Jesus is asking you, "Do you want to get well?" What is your answer? Give it to him straight. He can take it. He cares deeply.

This next mud hole is a tidy one—perfectionism. Settling for nothing less sounds almost holy. Jesus taught us to strive to be perfect as God is perfect (Matthew 5:48).

In this verse *perfect* means "complete" or "completeness."[3] God is complete. There is nothing lacking in his character, thoughts, words, and actions. Perfectionism doesn't strive to be more like God but to be the best above everyone. Its motive is not pure.

I know not everyone struggles with perfectionism in every area. My struggle has been to get everything perfect before guests come. Don't get any idea that my dinners were ooh-and-aah special. Since I even obsessed over everyday food, of course my husband, Gene, was less than enthused when I suggested having people over! Once I realized what I was doing and that no one ever noticed the little things I was fretting about, I was able to relax and not go nuts over meaningless details. Now I plan my menus to be delicious to my guests and still allow me to enjoy their company. No more Martha dinners for me (see Luke 10:38-42)! How about you? Where do you struggle with perfectionism?

How does perfectionism keep you from doing what God asks of you in that area?

Take a minute to talk with the Lord about what drives that perfectionism.

We'll end the week's study talking about procrastination. Ick. I know. Procrastination can be made acceptable because it is dripping in good intentions:

- ✦ "If I had time . . ."
- ✦ "If I weren't so tired . . ."
- ✦ "If my life weren't so confusing . . ."

Is procrastination something you have trouble getting victory over? What is your main difficulty?

- ❏ keeping the house clean
- ❏ keeping up with paperwork and bills

- ❏ planning meals and grocery shopping
- ❏ saying no to an overcommitted schedule
- ❏ home improvement projects started but not completed
- ❏ something else: _____

Procrastination is a pit of quicksand that keeps us from what God has for us. Years ago I read Donna Otto's book *Getting More Done in Less Time*. I learned the techniques and skills I needed to get my home in order. Now it runs fairly smoothly, and I have time to pursue the ministry God has given me. What area of procrastination could be keeping you from the next thing God has for you?

Dear Princess Unaware, I know this has been a hard chapter. If we were in the same small group, I would give you a hug right now! I am thrilled that you will be part of our journey and honored to have you as a sister princess!

Looking Back

How did the week go? Are you moving ahead with your King, or does he need to pull you out of a mud hole or two and clean you up? Will you listen as he teaches you how to avoid your most common traps? I know this process will not be easy, but trust your King. He is *for* you.

chapter two

Princess or Peasant?

The Princess Lives in the Reality of Her True Identity

A new dawn brightened Jess's outlook. She still had mud stains on her dress and her ankle was bruised, but she washed her hands and face in the clear, cold water of the brook and felt refreshed. She made a meager breakfast from the food her mother had packed.

My provisions must last the whole journey.

Jess continued onward, mindful that Pit Weasels could be anywhere. She hoped she would not encounter any more.

Midmorning, Jess's pace slowed. Her mind drifted happily into the clouds. She was jolted from her daze when she heard the pounding of hooves close behind her. She ran behind the nearest tree and peeked out from her hiding spot. A handsome young man on a regal stallion came into view, followed by a band of armed men.

"I know you're in there, Annabel!" he shouted. "I saw you dart for the forest."

Is he calling to me? Jess dared not even breathe. *Who is he? And who are those men with him, all dressed for battle?*

"Come on, Annabel. I need to get you home." The voice was sincere and strong.

Jess mustered courage and walked out into view, her chin set bravely. "Sir. My name is not Annabel," she said.

"I am sorry, young maiden," the young man said kindly. "I have mistaken you for one of my sisters. You do bear an uncanny resemblance, but alas, you are not her." He was turning his horse to leave when his eye caught a glimpse of Jess's gold medallion.

"Wait!" The young man dismounted. "You wear the crest of my family, but . . . it can't be. What is your name?"

More curious than frightened, Jess answered, "I am Jess of Kyrinn."

He looked again at the medallion and deeply into her face. "No . . ." the man said. "You are Princess Jessica of Calhedra, daughter of the King! You *are* my sister! We have been anticipating your arrival. But come quickly. I am on my way to battle, and I must keep going."

"What about my journey?"

"This *is* your journey."

Jess drew back. *Perhaps this is another trap like the Pit Weasels. Perhaps he is Scaly Red or Glittering Green in disguise.*

Seeing her reluctance, the man said, "I am Prince Cartier of Calhedra. Jessica, you *are* my sister. Look at the medallion around your neck. It is exactly like mine. The King, your other brothers and sisters, and I have been looking forward to your arrival for a long time."

She took a step closer and looked at the prince's medallion. He took it from his neck and held it out to her. She studied it. The crest was identical to hers. She looked into the man's eyes and saw a faint mirror of her own. She saw familiarity and belonging. She curtsied.

"Yes, I will go with you."

"Excellent. We will feast tonight at the cottage of Lady Penelope. You may spend the night in her cottage. My men and I will stand guard outside." The prince climbed onto his horse, offered his arm to Jess, and effortlessly lifted her up.

Princess. Am I really a princess? Jess clung to Prince Cartier as he and his knights rode hard to make up for lost time.

I hope Jess's question gets your attention and makes you think. Do you believe *you* are a princess? Are you living like a princess?

I presented this question to a group of women at a retreat. They were asked to write a response to the idea of being a princess. Many gave these statements:

+ I am a princess.
+ Praise the Lord. He loves me no matter what!
+ You are my Father in Heaven!

However, some of the women shared thoughts like these:

+ I don't feel much like a princess.
+ But I feel so haggard. Can this be how a princess feels?
+ I know God loves me, but I don't know why.

We are all meant to be princesses—daughters of the King who have a personal relationship with him. That is our heavenly Father's deepest desire. What is keeping you from having that kind of relationship with God—the Father, the

King? And what is keeping you from living as the strong, confident princess he designed you to be?

We will discuss the answers to these questions throughout this book. Right now, let's start with one answer—the lies we believe about ourselves. I want to expose these lies and replace them with the truth the King says about you. Once we know how God feels about us, we are ready to know him, to have good relationships, and to live the full life Jesus promised us (John 10:10).

I began my royal life as a child. I heard about Jesus, God's perfect Son, leaving his life in Heaven, suffering at the hands of men, dying on the cross, being resurrected, and ascending to Heaven—all to make me perfect and acceptable to God who loved me so much. In the simple language of a child, I prayed and told Jesus I was sorry for my sin and that I accepted all he did for me. I wanted to be his forever. So began my journey as a princess of the King.

The sad thing is, I didn't know I became a princess at that moment. For most of my royal life, I did not act like a princess. Why? Because no one told me that I was one! I still felt the same, not special. No one I knew well had a vital, intimate relationship with God that I could see. While I believed God and accepted his Son, God seemed distant. Any royalty I heard of lived across the ocean.

When I was older and started hearing words like *daughter of the King, fellow heirs with Christ*, and *princess*, I did not understand what they meant. No one treated me differently or special. Somehow I got the message that while my salvation was by faith and *not* because of the good things I did, God delighted in me only when I was "being good." Can anyone identify? And boy, I did not feel as if I delighted God! I fell short—all the time. Growing up as the oldest of five girls, my sibling-rivalry inclinations provided me with plenty of opportunity to fall short.

A few years later God started impressing on me the idea that I am royalty. He started helping me understand who I am and how he sees me—as a child of his because of Christ. This took lots of time, patience, and teaching on God's part, because my reality didn't match what he was trying to show me. If my Christian sisters and I were royalty, why were we all such a mess—full of self, pride, pettiness, gossip, guilt, and other negatives? Was the princess idea a lie—not from God, but maybe from well-meaning Bible teachers misinterpreting the Scriptures? Was this type of royal living for only a select few? Maybe it was for those who attained a level of spirituality that we normal women could never achieve because we weren't born into a family with generations of Christian heritage? What was up?

We're going to talk about that. We're going to see the truth in the Word. We're going to know that what God has said about us is not just for certain people we think are more deserving than we are. These words were written for all of us, and they are for all of us to believe. Once we believe something, we start living it.

The Princess Learns She Is Part of the Royal Family

First, if you have accepted Christ, you are part of God's family, and the benefits and privileges that are part of being in his family belong to you. Ephesians 2:19 says, "You are no longer foreigners and aliens, but fellow citizens with God's people and members of God's household."

Let that soak in.

I tell my friends when they come to visit, "I will get the first cup of coffee (or whatever) for you. After that you're welcome to get it yourself." I want them to be comfortable and feel like part of the family. Nothing does that like serving yourself. God not only wants us to feel like part of his family, he gave his best—Jesus—so we *can be* part of his family, with all the benefits, forever.

Now let's absorb two verses from Galatians: "If you belong to Christ, then you are Abraham's seed, and heirs according to the promise" (3:29). "So you are no longer a slave, but a son; and since you are a son, God has made you also an heir" (4:7). We aren't slaves stealing crumbs from the master's table. We *are* children of the King, part of his family. We didn't earn this. God made it available to us through his Son's obedience, death, and resurrection; and when we accept Christ we enter God's family.

The Princess Learns the King Loves Her

That takes us to the next truth: we are loved by God. "God showed how much he loved us by sending his one and only Son into the world so that we might have eternal life through him. This is real love—not that we loved God, but that he loved us and sent his Son as a sacrifice to take away our sins" (1 John 4:9, 10, *NLT*). Look at the sincerity of God's love—he gave everything to make us right with himself so we can have relationship with him.

What would you give to save someone from a life of destruction and death? Extra cash? Prayer? A place to live in your home? Maybe you would donate a kidney or bone marrow to save a life. But would you give up the person most precious to you? I wouldn't. But God did. That's how much he loves you. Believe this truth or not; that won't change the reality. God loves you—so much that he wants relationship with you not just here and now but forever in eternity.

First John 4:8 explains God's love this way: "God is love." For God, love is more than an emotion; it is his *being*. It is impossible for God not to love us.

Recently as I was checking in at a conference, I noticed the man helping me had a United States Marine Corps tattoo on his arm, half hidden by his shirt sleeve.

"Are you a former Marine?" I knew my mistake as soon as I had the words out.

"There is no such thing as a former Marine," he replied sternly, and then he smiled.

I quickly corrected myself. "I know better and I'm sorry. *Semper fi.*"

I do know better. My husband, Gene, is an ex-Marine, no longer in active duty. But *former Marine* implies that somehow all the "Marine" was taken out when the soldier left active duty. The Marines and their families I have met all agree it is impossible to take the Marine out of a Marine.

In a sense, God is like a Marine. Love is part of who he is. He can't take his love for us out of who he is. And because part of God's character is that he doesn't flip-flop but remains the same, we know he *always* wants what is best for us. So he doesn't promise us the best and then give us hand-me-downs. He always gives us what he knows is best for us. He doesn't switch out our blessing to someone he feels is more deserving.

If you're in hard circumstances, I know that's a big pill to choke down. I have been in hard times, and I have walked through hard things with close friends. Life is hard, but God is for us. We need only position ourselves to hear him and obey him and trust him. His heart aches more than ours.

A woman in my Bible study is a nurse. When one of her two-year-old patients needed a spinal tap, the child screamed and struggled to get free. My friend and other nurses had to strap and hold her down. Only after the test could the doctor make the diagnosis and prescribe the treatment the child desperately needed. The child had no idea why she had to go through this terrible pain and confinement; she did not understand she must go through it to bring healing to her body. My friend observed, "That's how God is with us sometimes." When we are going through excruciating times, our Father is there with us, holding and loving us.

The Princess Learns What to Wear

When we last read about Jess, dried mud covered her clothes, hardly a look for a princess. Before I became a princess, my clothes were covered in mud too—the mud of sin. Sin is all the things we think or do that are not obedient to or honoring to God. When I became a princess, Jesus washed me clean, but I didn't live in that reality. I still felt covered in mud.

When the apostle John wrote the book of Revelation, he included this awesome truth in his greeting to the churches: "To Him who loved us and washed us from our sins in His own blood, and has made us kings and priests to His God and Father, to Him be glory and dominion forever and ever" (1:5, 6, *NKJV*). The Father gave Jesus, his holy and perfect Son, to make *us* holy, perfect, and forgiven. These verses are rich in truth about who we are in Christ. First, Jesus loves us. How amazing is that! He wants our best. He cares deeply about us. He gave his life for us.

Next the verse states Jesus "washed us from our sins." The Greek word used here for *wash* means to bathe the whole person,[4] not just a part or her clothes. Because Jesus Christ gave his own blood for our sins, we are washed clean. We are as clean as we can be because of his love and blood. If this doesn't make you want to get down on your face before God in gratitude and humility, then I don't know what will.

Whatever past sin is coming to mind, if you have confessed it and asked forgiveness, it is gone; no shadow of a stain remains. God sees you as perfect. God tells us this clearly: "If we confess our sins, he is faithful and just and will forgive us our sins and purify us from all unrighteousness" (1 John 1:9). Soak in that phrase—"purify [you] from all unrighteousness." *Unrighteousness* means any "wrongfulness (of character, life or act)."[5] It covers everything in your life, no matter how small or how big, that is not in line with God and his Word. In the Bible God says what he means and means what he says. So if God says you are purified from *all* unrighteousness, that's what he means. Do you believe it? If not, be careful. You may be calling God a liar.

Precious Princess Unaware, if you have accepted all Jesus did for you, you are now dressed in righteous threads, "not having a righteousness of [your] own that comes from the law, but that which is through faith in Christ—the righteousness that comes from God and is by faith" (Philippians 3:9). *Righteousness* here is defined as "equitable (in character or act)" and by implication, "innocent, holy."[6] This is our reality. We are innocent and holy in God's sight. I love the way Joe Stowell explains this verse in his book *Simply Jesus*: "As Paul notes, being found in Him means that you and I have been wrapped in the very righteousness of Jesus Christ. Try to imagine the blinding, searing, white fire at the core of a new star blazing in the heavens. Now . . . what if you could take that searing radiance and just slip it over your shoulder like a robe? That just begins to describe what it means to have the righteousness of Jesus—the perfect, sinless, spotless Lamb of God—covering all of your life."[7]

If you are daily putting on an old garment stained with past sins and wearing it everywhere you go, stop! The past is history. Your reality is that you are a princess, and you have a glowing, new white outfit to wear.

The Princess Learns She Makes the King Smile

I believe all women deal with insecurity on some level. Often, the root of it is caring what others think about us, because of our pride. We may want to be part of the group. Or maybe we want to stand out from our coworkers so we get the promotion or seal the deal. Or we don't want our egos dented. All these motives are based on the desire to have others think well of us at all times. That smacks of idolatry—putting anything in God's place in our lives. The apostle Paul gave us great perspective here when he said, "I care very little if I am judged by you or by any human court; indeed, I do not even judge myself. My conscience is clear, but that does not make me innocent. It is the Lord who judges me" (1 Corinthians 4:3, 4). The only opinion we need to care about is God's.

We don't have to do amazing human tricks to get his attention or approval. I smile at the commercial in which the little dog keeps jumping higher and higher so his owner will notice, but all the while the owner is otherwise occupied and clueless. In your relationships, have you ever been like that dog? I have. It's exhausting. Finally, the Lord got through to me and said, "Enough. They don't see you, but I do." If you are his princess, God sees you. You are chosen and accepted by God. No jumping for attention required.

Take a look at Ephesians 1:4-14. Three times Paul states that we were chosen or predestined to be children of God by God's divine purpose. I know, some of you saw *chosen* and *predestined* and started having theological seizures or sat back in your chair with a smirk on your face, thinking, *How will Garrison get herself out of this one?* Some of you didn't react either way. No matter, you all can relax. I'm not here to join the theological debate. I'm simply taking the Word at its word—and it says God knew you would be his by his divine plan. God is *sovereign*, over all things.

I like shopping for clothes and accessories and home decor and putting together a look for myself or my home. However, just when I think I have the perfect purse, pair of shoes, or vase, I find something else I feel just as passionate about. I am ready to ditch my first choice and go for my latest find. I don't, but I am tempted. I'm not as committed as I thought.

God is not like that with us—crazy about us until he gets tired of us. Oh no! Let's read Ephesians 1:4: "He chose us in him before the creation of the world to be holy and blameless in his sight." God chose us before the world began, and he always wanted us to be perfect in his sight. Once again we see that the only opinion that matters is God's. The passage continues, "In love he predestined us to be adopted as his sons [and daughters] through Jesus Christ, in accordance with his pleasure and will" (vv. 4, 5). God picked us to be his daughters—his princesses—because that's what he wanted. Oh, that makes me smile.

Since we are chosen by God to be his princesses because it pleased him, it only makes sense that we are also accepted by him. I am a hard-headed woman, and I need proof before I believe something. I'm always asking Gene, "How do you know that?" or "Who told you that?" It drives him nuts. So, true to my nature, I want to show you in the Word *how I know* you are accepted: "Accept one another, then, just as Christ accepted you, in order to bring praise to God" (Romans 15:7). No more standing on the outside looking in. We are in, and we are in with the one who matters. I pray your heart is ready and able to receive the power of this truth that is *for you*. Let it sink in. Absorb it. God has accepted you because he wanted to. You make him smile. If you don't believe God accepts you, you don't believe God.

The Princess Learns She Can Talk to the King Anytime

Another truth we must absorb into our being if we are going to live as princesses is that we have total access to the King. Kings are not normally accessible. In centuries past they weren't even accessible to their wives or children. In the book of Esther, in an effort to save her people, Queen Esther boldly yet humbly went before the king—her husband—without being requested. She could have been killed for that brash action if the king had not extended his scepter to her.

That is not the case with us princesses. Because of what Christ did for us, we have access to our Father, the King. Jesus is always at God's right hand, ready to usher us in to talk with our Father. "So then, since we have a great High Priest who has entered heaven, Jesus the Son of God, let us hold firmly to what we believe. This High Priest of ours understands our weaknesses, for he faced all of the same testings we do, yet he did not sin. So let us come boldly to the throne of our gracious God. There we will receive his mercy, and we will find grace to help us when we need it most" (Hebrews 4:14-16, *NLT*). We—you and me, unworthy, insecure, sinning people that we are—are free to come to the throne of God anytime. As a princess, you have total access to your Father.

And we can come to our holy God with confidence. "So, friends, we can now—without hesitation—walk right up to God, into 'the Holy Place.' Jesus has cleared the way by the blood of his sacrifice, acting as our priest before God. The 'curtain' into God's presence is his body. So let's do it—full of belief, confident that we're presentable inside and out" (Hebrews 10:19-22, *The Message*). Are you confident you are presentable inside and out? We can know it. The Bible says it, so it's true.

The 2005 movie *Pride and Prejudice* is one of my family's favorites (except for Gene). Near the end, Elizabeth finally starts to see Mr. Darcy's true character instead of who she had assumed him to be in her quick judgments. She realizes all the brave and costly acts Mr. Darcy did for her family because of his love for her. He had no promise she would love him in return, especially in light of her previous scathing refusal of his marriage proposal. Yet he did all he could to help her family.

In one of the last scenes of the movie, Elizabeth can't sleep. She gets up just before dawn and wanders about on her family's vast property, lost in thought. In the predawn light she sees Mr. Darcy striding toward her. He is not his usual put-together self. His shirt is unbuttoned to reveal just the right amount of chest hair (come on, you know what I'm talking about!). They meet and fumble their words as they each try to explain their past behaviors. Then with sincere, puppy-dog eyes, Mr. Darcy says, "You must know . . . surely, you must know it was all for you."[8] Of course, all female hearts are melting.

Through the inspired words of the Bible, our heavenly Father says to us, "Surely, you must know it was all for you." The apostle Paul asked, "What, then, shall we say in response to this? If God is for us, who can be against us? He who did not spare his own Son, but gave him up for us all—how will he not also, along with him, graciously give us all things?" (Romans 8:31, 32).

Have you responded to your Father's love and all he has done for you? Have you taken a moment to tell him how much you appreciate it and, yes, you want to be his princess? If you have never had this conversation with him, this is the perfect time. Here is an example of a prayer you can use to start your relationship with God. It is only a model, so don't be afraid to use your own words:

Dear God,

Thank you for loving me so much—more than I can imagine! Thank you for giving your perfect Son so I can be forever with you. You and I both know I've done things I'm not proud of. I confess them to you now. I want to live the life Christ died to give me and that you planned for me. So I ask for your forgiveness and cleansing. Only you can make me clean and dress me in a robe of Christ's brilliant righteousness. That's what I want. Thank you, Father! I love you.

Dear Princess Unaware, when you have given your life to Jesus, you are a princess of the most holy King. How will that change your thinking? (I wonder how Princess Jessica is adjusting to her new identity—going from peasant to princess in one afternoon?) That is you too, princess! Whether you've just acquired your new identity or just recognized it afresh, what will you do with it? Will you deny it or own it? Those are your only two choices. Your thoughts and actions will show what you choose.

If you choose to deny your true identity, you can pretty much expect more of what life has been offering you—frustration, guilt, failed resolutions, and lack of fulfillment. If you choose to own your true identity, however, you will have the ride of your life—waking up each morning knowing that your Father is smiling on you and loving you, no matter what. Life won't be easy or perfect, but you will have peace that you have never known. You will have purpose and direction even in the small things of life. You will be secure in who you are, no longer trying to impress others or be someone you're not. Through all this you will be maturing into the strong, confident princess you are—no longer a princess unaware.

At the back of this book is a Royal Truths section. Go now to page 273 and write what you learned about yourself today and what you learned about your Father. Include the Scripture references that state the truths you learned. Whether you choose to write a lot or just a little, my desire is for you to have the essential truths of what you learn in one place that you can easily refer back to. This will help the truths get into your mind and, thus, into your life.

Finding the Fabulous

 ## Looking Ahead

This week is crucial to the rest of the material in the book. Unless we own the truth that we are princesses of the King, we will not have the determination we need as we journey with Princess Jessica. We have many exciting adventures ahead! No matter where you are in this process of believing, will you put yourself in a posture to hear from God? By *posture* I mean getting your heart and will ready to hear from God and to work through your stuff, listening to truth and absorbing his Word in order to let it be the reality you live in. Ask him to help you be teachable, no matter what you're feeling. Ask him to help your mind and heart absorb, understand, and accept his truth and keep you moving ahead with him, no matter what may try to stop you.

✦ ✦ ✦ ✦ ✦ ✦ ✦ ✦ ✦ ✦ ✦

DAY ONE: Princess Who?

How are you doing with this notion that you might not be who you thought you were—an ordinary woman living an ordinary life?

If you have accepted Christ's sacrifice for you and become a daughter of the King, record that in the Royal Truths section at the back of the book. If you had been with us on the retreat where you were asked to write a response to the truth that you are a princess, what would you have written?

I don't always feel very royal. Some days I feel more like the scullery maid than the princess. I clean my own house (yes, my princesses help), cook most of our meals, do the ironing, and because of all this I dare not get a manicure. It would be undone overnight. No, my life is not made of the stuff of royalty. I'm sure yours isn't either. That is why we need to change our way of thinking about what it means to be a princess of the King.

How do you think a princess should live? How should she present herself to the watching world? What behaviors are not befitting a princess? What characteristics exemplify a princess?

I admire Barbara and Laura Bush. Each of them handled her first-lady role with grace, integrity, and political savvy. Name a woman you think wears her title of "royalty" well. Feel free to include any of America's first ladies, since we don't have a royal line.

Now name a princess of the King who wears her title of royalty well, maybe someone who is your role model. This person can be well known or someone you know personally.

Are you starting to get a princess picture? A strong, confident princess lives from the inside out. She knows she belongs to the King, and she lives like it, regardless of her life's circumstances.

Think About It

What do you think is keeping you from owning the truth and being the strong, confident princess? Can you lay that roadblock at God's feet? Let him have it. It doesn't befit a princess.

Years ago I emceed a women's event at our church. We hosted a well-known Christian speaker, and I was thrilled to get to know her. Before one session as I sat next to her, chatting, her daughter walked up to us. All of a sudden I found myself scooted down the pew to make room for the daughter to sit between us. *Oh . . . OK, her daughter comes first.* While I was a bit startled, I understood that this speaker held her daughter near and that the daughter had uninterrupted access to her mother.

Ephesians 2:11-22 tells us that God also holds us near and that we have uninterrupted access to our Father. If you are not of the Jewish race, you are a Gentile. The Jews are God's chosen people. However, we see in these verses that God is bringing the Gentiles into the family too.

Read verse 13. What was your position?

What is your current position?

How did you get there?

Try to put words to what this truth means to you.

I love that phrase *brought near.* Allow me one warm, fuzzy moment. *I have been brought near to God.* Yes, I love that. I was out in the cold, gray, lonely place, and now because of Christ's blood I am fast-forwarded right into God's warm, loving, gracious presence.

Read Ephesians 2:19. Being part of a household implies privileges and responsibilities. What are a few privileges of being part of your household?

I'd say one of the best privileges of being part of our household is access to the kitchen. I do my best to keep yummy and healthy food in the fridge and pantry. If you are a member of our household, you have access to a snack whenever you need one (unless it's ten minutes before dinner).

What are a few responsibilities of being part of your household?

As I mentioned, my girls and I share the housecleaning. All members of the household are responsible for picking up and cleaning up after themselves. It's what we do to keep our home comfortable and functioning smoothly.

Throughout this book we will discuss many privileges and responsibilities of being in

God's household. Right now, if you can, name one privilege and one responsibility of being in God's household. I want to gently remind you that your answer needs to be based on God's Word and not a teaching of a denomination or a person.

✦ ✦ ✦ ✦ ✦ ✦ ✦ ✦ ✦ ✦ ✦

DAY TWO: I Am Loved

I remember the shocking moment on our honeymoon when I realized my new husband could irritate me. I came out of the bathroom and heard the TV. Gene was watching one of the morning news shows. (Remember, this was twenty-four years ago, and TV was not on all the time, everywhere, as it seems to be now.) I thought, *Why does he have the TV on this early?* The noise irritated me. This is a tiny example of a situation where romantic love is not going to get us through something difficult.

If real love isn't about romantic feelings, what is it about? Read 1 John 4:9, 10 again. From that passage how would you describe love?

Real love is about what is best for the other person, even if it costs us. What would you give to save someone else from a life of destruction and death?

If you wanted to explain God's reason for sending Jesus to earth, what would you say? We needed the perfect, unblemished Lamb (Jesus) to conquer Satan once and for all. But *why* did God do it? Why not let the human race get what we deserve—eternity without God?

Think About It

God wants what is best for us because he loves us. He knows a perfect relationship with him is what is best for us. It is only possible because Jesus gave his life to make us perfect and acceptable to God. Read 1 John 4:8. How can you get your mind around the truth that "God is love"?

God is always looking on you with delight (Zephaniah 3:17). God does not change; he doesn't wake up in a bad mood some days and decide to frown on you. No, he loves you every day. You can't make him love you more or less. Write the words of Zephaniah 3:17 on an index card to help you remember this truth.

Recall a time when you were discouraged because you felt God was richly blessing someone else and just shaking out the crumbs for you. Come on, be honest. We've all been there.

Now, knowing the truth about how God feels about you, how can you better process the lie from Satan that says God is holding out on you?

Read Genesis 3. In verse 1 what is Satan's method of operation for tempting Eve?

How did Eve deal with the doubt Satan placed in her mind (vv. 2, 3)?

Instead of sticking with what God had told her, Eve tried to reason out the situation on her own. She "saw that the fruit of the tree was good for food and pleasing to the eye, and also desirable for gaining wisdom" (v. 6). How did Eve respond to her own "wisdom"?

What were the results when Eve trusted her reasoning skills based on what she could see (vv. 7, 8, 12-24)?

Since we are only human, we can't see the whole picture. Like Eve, we don't know what we don't know. Eve did not have a clue that taking a bite of the fruit would introduce sin to mankind. She did not know that sin would cause separation from God, with whom she'd enjoyed a perfect relationship up to this point. She did not know sin would bring eventual physical death and then an eternity separated from God. She didn't see God's big picture. But she chose not to trust what she *did* know—what God had said—and instead trusted in the lies and temptation of the serpent.

Think of a time you were in Eve's position. You knew God would not allow the thing you wanted to do, but you couldn't see what the harm would be. How did you respond? What were the results?

The strong, confident princess listens and obeys, even though she would rather do things her way. She knows that she is loved by the King and that she can trust him.

♦ ♦ ♦ ♦ ♦ ♦ ♦ ♦ ♦ ♦ ♦

DAY THREE: The Princess Learns to Listen to the King

No one can tattle better than a sister. I know—I come from a family of four sisters (no brothers), and I have three daughters (no sons). Getting a sister in trouble with mom and dad is the best kind of revenge.

Princesses also have to deal with a tattletale—Satan. "Then I heard a loud voice shouting across the heavens, 'It has come at last—salvation and power and the Kingdom of our God, and the authority of his Christ. For the accuser of our brothers and sisters has been thrown down to earth—the one who accuses them before our God day and night'" (Revelation 12:10, *NLT*). As if we don't beat ourselves up enough, Satan is always around to lend a hand. But this is the thing you must know in order to move on, dear Princess Unaware—we are clean before God. Our part is to tell God what we have done wrong, that we know it was wrong, and that we are sorry. Then God forgives us because of Jesus. "If we confess our sins, he is faithful and just and will forgive us our sins and purify us from all unrighteousness" (1 John 1:9).

You are now clean. Satan has nothing on you. The Lord says, "Their sins and lawless acts I will remember no more" (Hebrews 10:17). We are wearing garments of righteousness. Imagine yourself taking off your muddy dress and trading it in for a beautiful gown of righteousness—a gift from Jesus. How do you feel in your brilliant gown?

That gown is yours to wear forever. No one can take it from you. Read Romans 8:35-39. List everything that cannot keep us from Jesus' love.

Can you think of anything not on that list?

One more dose of security in Christ. Read John 10:27-30. In verse 28, what three truths does Christ state about his sheep (princesses)?

What final seal of truth does Christ give in verses 29, 30?

Are you starting to see how unprincesslike it is for you to keep lugging around all your junk from the past (or even from this morning)? Unload it all at the feet of your Father. Jesus came to take care of your sin, so you have no more guilt or condemnation (Romans 8:1).

 ## One More Thing

I want to clarify this—sin is sin. Deal with the sin God is showing you. Don't read more into these questions than what God shows you. I'm not looking for you to come up with a deep, dark past. If you have one, deal with it with Christ and let's move on together. If you don't, your sin still needs to be dealt with. No princess is better or worse than another.

As I mentioned, all my life I have lived with females dripping with estrogen. All the drama of who talked to whom, what was said, how she responded, what they were thinking, why we weren't included . . . ugh. And I'm not talking only about junior high. I see this in the relationships of adult women. We are way too concerned about what the other princesses think about us. (If you feel you are beyond the girlfriend drama, think again. Do you try to listen in on conversations? Do you get caught up in office politics so you can further your career? Do you feel smug when someone is having a bad hair day?)

The root of all the drama is often our insecurity. We not only want to be part of the group, we want to know that we are firmly established in the group so we won't be booted out on a whim. The root of insecurity is not trusting God and believing instead that we must make a way for ourselves because God is not going to take care of us.

In Ephesians 1:1-9 Paul talks about the generous, free gifts God has lavished on us—all because God loves us and he wanted to bless us. The whole theme of this chapter is Paul saying, "Hey, look at all God has done to convince you he loves you." Even the words Paul used convey the extent of how God feels about us. Let's go through each verse and note specific words Paul used to describe what God has given us and done for us.

Verse 3

Verse 4

Verse 5

Verse 6

Verses 7, 8

Verse 9

If you will think often and throughout the day on these verses, they will change what you believe about yourself. We are holy—let it sink in. We are blameless—no one can condemn us.

Princess Unaware, are you starting to walk stronger and taller? Is your load a little lighter? You are a princess of the King. Drop your insecurities at his feet. He made you, designed you, and planned a life of specific good works for you to do (Psalm 139; Ephesians 2:10; Jeremiah 29:11). How could a perfect, sovereign God mess up making you? It's impossible. You're cool with God.

One More Thing

I know this is a process, but right now place yourself in a posture to agree with God on these issues. No more excuses. He knows what you are ready to deal with. He won't rush you.

✦ ✦ ✦ ✦ ✦ ✦ ✦ ✦ ✦ ✦ ✦

DAY FOUR: The Princess Learns to Talk with the King

Never in human history has on-demand communication been so possible. The other day when I was shopping, I received a text from Kelsey telling me something she couldn't wait to say. Just now as I am writing, my computer told me I had incoming e-mail. It was from Katie, who was just e-mailed by Kerry, who is at school. We were all discussing our weekend plans. My point is, I am accessible to my girls anytime in any manner they want to communicate. God is that way too. He is ready and able to communicate with us all the time in the way that suits us best. Just as I delight in hearing from my girls, even more does God delight in hearing from us. We have total, confident, bold access to our Father.

Read Hebrews 4:14-16. In the Old Testament, God designated priests to present offerings and sacrifices on behalf of the people. The high priest, however, was the only one allowed to enter the Holy of Holies of the temple to make a yearly sacrifice to atone for the people's sins. In these verses we learn that Jesus is our high priest. The sacrifice he made, however, was "once for all" (Hebrews 7:27). Now Jesus stands with us before God as our high priest. He makes us perfect, acceptable, and ready for relationship with God. What other experience does Christ bring to his role as our high priest (Hebrews 4:15)?

What difference does that make? How does that fact impact the way we come to God and talk with him?

I love the way *The Message* states Hebrews 10:19-22: "So, friends, we can now—without hesitation—walk right up to God, into 'the Holy Place.' Jesus has cleared the way by the blood of his sacrifice, acting as our priest before God. The 'curtain' into God's presence is his body. So let's do it—full of belief, confident that we're presentable inside and out."

What does this passage say we can confidently do?

What makes this possible?

What do we need to know to approach God with confidence?

Jesus has done the hard work for us. He lived a perfect life, suffered, gave his life, conquered Satan—all so we can have a relationship with him and the Father. We just need to believe and accept Christ and then "walk right up to God"—knowing who we are, his princesses—and start a conversation with him. He is waiting.

Read Romans 8:31, 32. How have your thoughts about your true identity changed?

If you are still not able to accept your identity as a princess of the King, how do you reconcile these verses with your unbelief?

Dear Princess Unaware, we have done some hard work this week. Are these truths starting to get into your thinking, your being? Are you soaking up the atmosphere of love, acceptance, and forgiveness that God has for you? Don't forget to note the important truths you learned this week in the Royal Truths section!

 Looking Back

Are you beginning to see yourself differently? Maybe you're more aware of Christ at your side as you approach God's throne? Maybe you sat at Jesus' feet, chattering about your day or just enjoying his presence and his love. Maybe you have snuggled on his lap, letting him heal the wounds of your day or your life. This is the place he wants you to live—in his presence, soaking in his love, knowing what he has done for you and why, and then boldly, freely living the life he planned for you and being the person he designed you to be.

chapter three

The King and I

The Princess Knows Her Father

"Oh, I never thought I would see the day!" Lady Penelope's kind, wavering voice held years of wisdom. "Princess Jessica—coming back to the castle!"

Jessica's cheeks flushed. "I still can't believe I'm a real princess."

"Let's get you used to looking like royalty. Get those ratty clothes off. We'll pour you a nice warm bath. Then you may have your choice of silks or taffetas—clothes fit for a princess! I still have some from when your sisters used to summer here."

While Lady Penelope pulled delicate summer dresses out of a wardrobe, Jessica slipped behind the dressing screen and into the huge washtub of hot water. Her sore muscles melted like candle wax. How very tired she was!

After some time Lady Penelope said, "I think you'll be lovely in the blue silk." Then she broached the topic of the King. "Uh . . . dear, has Cartier mentioned your Father yet?"

"Not very much." Jessica was a bit timid to learn about the powerful figure she was told was her Father. Only a few days ago, she had left her humble family and peasant cottage life. How she ached to be at her mother's table, sharing tea and cookies with the parents she knew.

"Your Father, the King, is an amazing man," said Lady Penelope.

"I'm sure he is," said Jessica. She emerged from the tub and dressed in the blue silk garment Lady Penelope had selected for her. "That is part of what scares me."

"Your Father doesn't want to scare you. He loves you."

"My parents assured me of the same . . . from this book." Jessica pulled the book from her satchel. Lady Penelope began teaching her about the King from its pages.

✦ ✦ ✦ ✦ ✦ ✦ ✦ ✦ ✦ ✦ ✦

Princess Jessica is eager to know the King, her Father. She must learn about him from the book and spend time with him in relationship. To know our heavenly Father, we also need to see for ourselves what God says about himself in his book—the Bible—and develop a relationship with him.

Do you really know God, or do you just know the idea of God you have created over your lifetime? Knowing the truth about God is important because it is the basis for how we will live our lives—how we make decisions, relate to others, and do our work. Personally knowing God affects every part of life.

You might be tempted to go to the world for answers about God. The *world* is anything that is not from God and his Word. The world's answers only make our issues messier and our baggage heavier. Many counterfeit gods exist in this world, and all their positive-thinking-live-your-best-life-law-of-attraction-the-secret philosophy will not change us or our lives. But knowing our Father's character will give us hope, perspective, and freedom from all the junk we are carrying.

The King Is Love

The first thing Princess Jessica will learn about her Father is "God is love" (1 John 4:8). What does that mean? Why doesn't the verse say, "God is loving"? First, let's define *love*. The Greek word for *love* used here is *agape*. It means "affection or benevolence."[9] Agape love is not a fluffy emotion that makes God feel good. It is God's benevolence in giving everything he could for our benefit. *Benevolence* means the "disposition to do good."[10] God's love for us ensures that he always does what is best for us.

I know that is hard to understand and accept, especially when we or our loved ones are going through hard times. Unfortunately, the common wisdom in the Western world often associates blessing with a life of ease. We miss the powerful truth that in trying circumstances we get to know God in a way that we could not know him in times of ease. Difficulties allow us to be in a posture to know God's heart more intimately. And isn't our goal in life to know God—not to sail through life with no troubles, perfect health, a hefty bank account, and superficial relationships? Do you have a friend or family member with whom you have gone through hard times? Wasn't that relationship deepened by those circumstances?

The Ryrie Study Bible notes, "*Agape* characterizes God (1 John 4:18) and what He manifested in the gift of His Son (John 3:16). It is more than mutual affection; it expresses unselfish esteem of the object loved. Christ's love for us is undeserved and without thought of return."[11] Yes, God loves us even though we never will be deserving or worthy.

God expresses his love for us through unselfishly regarding us highly, with respect and admiration. He gives love freely—without thought of return. God values us—prizes us. "God is so rich in mercy, and he loved us so much, that even though we were dead because of our sins, he gave us life when he raised Christ from the dead. (It is only by God's grace that you have been saved!)" (Ephesians 2:4, 5, *NLT*).

God's Love Never Runs Out

This love of God is plentiful. "Rend your heart and not your garments. Return to the Lord your God, for he is gracious and compassionate, slow to anger and abounding in love, and he relents from sending calamity" (Joel 2:13). His love for us abounds. We cannot use up all the love God has for us, no matter how hard we try.

An excellent example of this is in Luke 15:11-32. Here Jesus tells a story (called a parable) to answer the grumblings of religious leaders (the Pharisees and scribes) because Jesus was hanging out with tax collectors and sinners. (That's us too.) In the parable, a father had two sons. The older son faithfully labored for his father; however, the younger son decided he wanted his share of his inheritance right away. "Not long after that, the younger son got together all he had, set off for a distant country and there squandered his wealth in wild living" (v. 13). Eventually the younger son became tired of feeding pigs to try to get by, and he came home to put things right with dad and hopefully be taken back as one of his father's hired servants. Verse 20 says poignantly, "But while he was still a long way off, his father saw him and was filled with compassion for him; he ran to his son, threw his arms around him and kissed him."

Dear Princess Unaware, no matter what kind of wild living you have done, God is ready and waiting to pour out his love on you. "How great is the love the Father has lavished on us, that we should be called children of God! And that is what we are!" (1 John 3:1).

Recently I ate dinner in the nicest restaurant I have ever visited. I was in a party of twenty. When our entrées were ready, twenty waiters came into our private room. One stood behind each guest, and on signal every other waiter placed a plate in front of a guest. Ten seconds later on signal, the other waiters placed their plates in front of their guests. Within thirty seconds all twenty of us had been served. The food was incredible. I wanted to savor each bite for an hour. It was a lavish evening.

God lavishes us with his love even more. Whether I am in a fancy restaurant or at home washing dishes, I am wrapped in God's love. He always wants my best and works for my best. He always smiles on me and delights in me (Zephaniah 3:17).

Finally, nothing can keep us from God's love. "I am convinced that neither death nor life, neither angels nor demons, neither the present nor the future, nor any powers, neither height nor depth, nor anything else in all creation, will be able to separate us from the love of God that is in Christ Jesus our Lord" (Romans 8:38, 39). That list includes everything that we might fear would keep God's love from us. The truth is, nothing can get in the way or persuade God not to love us. His love is a done deal.

God's Love Covers Our Issues

Now let's plug the reality of God's love into some of our issues. Start with insecurity. God's loving us means he highly esteems us—adores us. Now think about it. If God adores us, if we have his constant attention, why do we need the approval of anyone else? Why do we worry about others' opinions?

My bathrobe is the new microterry type of fabric. Thick and soft, it is my ultimate comfort clothing. When I put it on, I feel warm and cozy. The self-tie enables me to cinch it up snug, and the collar comes high up on my neck to keep out a chill. God's love for us is like a warm, cozy robe. It keeps out the insecurities and lies that Satan whispers in our ears.

Now apply God's love generously to the issues of fear, loneliness, and guilt. Because we are in God's constant love, we don't need to fear anything. He has our lives covered. Are you still hanging on to past guilt? Why? "There is now no condemnation for those who are in Christ Jesus" (Romans 8:1). God is not condemning you for your past sin. He has forgiven you. Hanging on to past guilt brings condemnation, and that is from Satan. Do you see how all of our issues roll off when we are covered in the love of God?

Those of you who, like me, analyze ideas into the ground might have wondered, *Yes, God loves me, but does he like me? I'm different from so many women I know. I'm not everyone's flavor. So does God like me?* The answer to that is yes! Psalm 139:13-16 teaches us this truth. God made you just the way he wanted you to be. "I thank you, High God—you're breathtaking! Body and soul, I am marvelously made! I worship in adoration—what a creation!" (Psalm 139:14, *The Message*). God doesn't make mistakes, and you are not a mistake. God planned the intricacies of your personality; they are his desire for you to be the unique person he planned you to be from the beginning of time.

The King Is Faithful

"He is the Rock, his works are perfect, and all his ways are just. A faithful God who does no wrong, upright and just is he" (Deuteronomy 32:4). God is faithful. We can trust him. That's what he wants from us—our trust—our faith in him and his Son. If we can absorb these truths into our minds, we will be transformed.

Let's do some life application. If God is faithful and he loves us, why do we worry or fear? Why do we think and act as if we are going through life alone and it's all up to us? God knows our financial need, how difficult our child is, our health issues . . . He knows. He is faithful. Because God is who he is, it is impossible for us to be out of his care. God is incapable of not thinking about us. "For whoever touches you touches the apple of his eye" (Zechariah 2:8). We are in the center of God's vision always.

I know these truths about God, but sometimes when it's time to apply a truth to my situation, I doubt. Yep, I doubt. I don't like admitting this to you. Sometimes I say God is faithful, but my anxiety reveals my doubt. I think, *Yeah, I know God said this truth and that truth, but my situation is different.* Have you ever been there?

God requires action on our part. Knowing that God is faithful to help me in a situation doesn't take me out of the situation. No, I must let God faithfully stretch me and work changes in me; I must do the next thing he shows me in the situation—things I might not want to do and don't think I should have to do. God says, "You can do this. We will do it together, but we've got to do it."

Moses experienced God's faithfulness in ways like no one else. God gave Moses an "impossible job" (see Exodus 3, 4)—but not impossible with God Almighty. Moses had God's calling. God spoke directly to him, telling him what he wanted Moses to do. God gave Moses words to say and signs to prove to Israel, Pharaoh, and Moses himself that God had sent him and was with him. Moses needed to step out, believing God would be faithful. It wouldn't be easy or fun, but if he really believed God is faithful, he had to do what God instructed him to do.

A scene from *Indiana Jones and the Last Crusade* illustrates God's faithfulness and how we princesses walk by faith. In the movie, Indiana Jones must find the Holy Grail and bring it back to save his dying father by the Grail's rumored healing powers. (I know this isn't biblical.) Indiana comes upon a chasm that is impossible to get across, but he must cross to continue on. He recites the clues obtained from his father's notes.

"It's . . . a leap of faith,"[12] he concludes. He steps out into the chasm, into thin air. The moment he does so, what was an invisible stone bridge materializes (becomes visible) beneath his foot. Astonished and relieved, Indiana Jones crosses and completes his mission.

Princess, you too must step out on what our Father has told us. It might be scary, but he is faithful to provide the strength you need and make the way for you to obey. This doesn't mean life will always go as you'd like. It does mean that God has allowed whatever is happening in your life, and it is for your good. In the process you will know your Father better and become more of the princess he planned for you to be. Dozens of people in the Bible experienced the truth in this verse: "God will do this, for he is faithful to do what he says, and he has invited you into partnership with his Son, Jesus Christ our Lord" (1 Corinthians 1:9, *NLT*).

God is faithful in your circumstances. He is always working on your behalf. Do you believe it?

The King Is Sovereign

God's *sovereignty*, his "exercise of power over his creation,"[13] is key to our relying on God's faithfulness. The Bible is full of verses stating this and examples of God's sovereignty. "When they heard the report, all the believers lifted their voices together in prayer to God: 'O Sovereign Lord, Creator of heaven and earth, the sea, and everything in them'" (Acts 4:24, *NLT*). What a great reminder to us as we start to pray—"O Sovereign Lord."

Let's put this together: God exercises power over his creation, and because he loves us (wants our best, highly esteems us) and is faithful to us (always in control of what comes into our lives), the power he exercises over us must be for our good and in love.

Whew. Don't we feel better? This world—our world—is not spinning out of control. It's in the control of our loving, faithful, almighty, all-wise Father. He will always give us or do for us what is best. "If they ask for a fish, do you give them a snake? Of course not! So if you sinful people know how to give good gifts to your children, how much more will your heavenly Father give good gifts to those who ask him" (Matthew 7:10, 11, *NLT*). Whatever comes into our lives is allowed for our good by our sovereign, heavenly Father.

Our daughters are at stages of life when what they go through seems to affect everyone. Our oldest daughter has been on her own for about three years. She is doing great. (Those who read *Queen Mom* will smile with me!) Our second daughter is nineteen and in her second year at community college before she moves away for her junior and senior years. Gene and I have moved her boundaries way out so she can experience the reality of her decisions and their consequences while she is still at home. This leaves our youngest, age fourteen, the only one still being fully parented. Oh, the rub! I do feel for her. While we don't agree with all the decisions the older girls make, we don't interfere unless necessary. At this point the consequences of their decisions are perfect teachers. However, we are still quite involved in Kerry's life, and that means sometimes her life looks boring compared to her sisters'. Gene and I do what we believe is best for her. While we are not omniscient (having perfect knowledge) as God is, we are her parental authority, and we answer to God for the way we parent her—whether it's fun for her or not.

Can we rest in the truth that our sovereign, omniscient heavenly Father is doing what is best for us? At times he may enlarge our boundaries to allow us to learn from our decisions, and at other times he may set our boundaries close, but we know he is always doing what he knows is best for us from his pure motive of love.

The King Always Listens

The last characteristic of God we will discuss in this chapter answers a question that is always on my mind when I am talking with someone: Are you listening? Being heard is a core need I have. I love the fact that God hears me—all the time. "Everything God does is right—the trademark on all his works is love. God's there, listening for all who pray, for all who pray and mean it. He does what's best for those who fear him—hears them call out, and saves them. God sticks by all who love him, but it's all over for those who don't" (Psalm 145:17-20, *The Message*).

In Daniel 10 we learn much about prayer. In that chapter Daniel, a Jewish exile, has seen a vision from God that "concerned a great war" (v. 1). Daniel was so affected by the vision that he "mourned for three weeks" (v. 2), with prayer and fasting. Then an angel visited Daniel to tell him the meaning of his vision. The angel's message gives us invaluable insight into how our prayers are received by God and into Heaven.

First, God hears us in real time. The angel told Daniel, "Do not be afraid, Daniel. Since the first day that you set your mind to gain understanding and to humble yourself before your God, your words were heard, and I have come in response to them" (v. 12). Not only does God hear us, he hears us as soon as we pray; and he puts in motion the plan for the answer to our prayer. This passage from Daniel goes on to tell of the angel's supernatural battle with an evil angel and the delay it caused. God was working, but the battle took time.

Next, we learn from the angel that prayer is not bringing God over to our way of thinking; prayer allows God to bring us to his way of thinking. How convicting! The angel acknowledged that Daniel had set his heart on understanding. Daniel wanted to know God's plan. He was seeking God to know him and his thoughts on this vision.

The angel also said Daniel's heart was set on humbling himself before God. The Hebrew word used here for *humble* means "looking down" and to "chasten self, deal hardly with."[14] This does not mean we are to hurt ourselves or adopt a form of self-hatred in an attempt to be heard by God. It does mean that we understand who we are and who God is. When we do that, we see that we are naturally sinful and have nothing in ourselves that gives us position before God (Ephesians 2:1-9). We are not in that humble posture if we stand before God like spoiled, stubborn children, stomping our little feet and demanding our way.

Remember from the previous chapter that we come to our Lord boldly, with confidence, because of who we are in Christ (princesses). I like to picture God on his throne and me standing in front of him (or sometimes sitting at his feet) in my glowing white robe, with Christ standing next to me, interceding on my behalf. I don't need to worry what God will think of me or that he will be mad. I have freedom of relationship to be myself and express myself.

The strong, confident princess comes to God, earnestly seeking him and his will, humbly and with confidence. Because of who she is in Christ, she knows she is heard.

But this is not the last word on prayer. We barely broached the topic. Just because we pray humbly, earnestly, and boldly with confidence through Christ does not mean we get what we are asking for. It does mean we are heard by our loving Father and that he will do what he knows is best for us and our loved ones. Jesus feels our pain and sorrow. The Holy Spirit is praying for us. "The Holy Spirit helps us in our weakness. For example, we don't know what God wants us to pray for. But the Holy Spirit prays for us with groanings that cannot be expressed in words" (Romans 8:26, *NLT*). We are covered.

As I was working on this chapter, I received some bad news regarding an incredible opportunity for ministry that had been guaranteed to me. I had been waiting patiently, trusting it would come about as I had been told. Then I received an e-mail stating that the opportunity was not going to take place. God brought to mind the words I had written the previous day concerning prayer:

- *Come to me humbly.*
- *Talk to me earnestly.*
- *Know you are standing boldly, confidently before me dressed in Christ's righteousness with him at your side.*
- *You are heard. I see you. I love you. I am smiling on you and singing over you. I've got this covered.*

Wow. What a difference. I experienced not only peace but also physical energy and strength.

Dear Princess Unaware, God is everything we need for our fears, insecurities, guilt, and all our other issues. Plug that into what's ailing you today.

Finding the Fabulous

Every princess needs a king. The king is the foundation for the credibility of the kingdom. Knowing God, the King, will show you the awesomeness of his kingdom and the honor, blessings, and responsibilities of being his princess. Take your time with your study this week. This week will be crucial for you to fully understand what it means to be a princess. Prayerfully let God speak to you, Princess Unaware. Through his Word, get to know your Father.

Looking Ahead

This week as you lie down to sleep each night, think for a moment on God's amazing love for you. He loves you *and* he likes you! Remember to use the Royal Truths section to make special note of what you are learning about God and yourself.

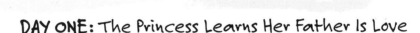

DAY ONE: The Princess Learns Her Father Is Love

God's love for us is unfathomable to our finite minds. However, I want us to try to understand its many facets, trusting God to speak to us through one or more of them this week.

How would you define *agape love*?

Now define *benevolence*.

Using these definitions and everything we have talked about so far, explain God's love for you. In your own words, what does God's love look like?

Sometimes we make life too hard. I love the way God speaks directly to us in the Bible. The following short verse gives us one instruction and two characteristics of God: "Give thanks to the LORD, for he is good; his love endures forever" (1 Chronicles 16:34). God's love for you will never end. Have you ever felt you were testing the love of someone to the limits and it might run out? Were you the "wild child" teenager? Or were you the teen who feared your parents' love was finite, so you didn't test it?

Jesus told a story about a family with both types of kids. Read Luke 15:11-32. Which son do you most identify with? Why?

If you identify more with the wild child, have you repented and come back to your Father? If no, what is stopping you?

Now read verse 20 again. Your Father is looking for you, waiting for you to come back so he can run to you and throw his arms around you. He is filled with compassion for you. Will you get up and go to your Father? What does your Father's enduring love mean to you as you come to him? If this verse touches a tender part in your heart, write it on an index card so God can continually use it to remind you of his compassion for you.

If you have repented and returned to your Father, have you accepted his forgiveness, or are you still trying to earn his love? Explain.

Read verse 29. What motivated the older brother, Mr. Perfect?

The older son wasn't serving his father because he loved him and wanted to please him. He wanted something in return for his hard work and faithfulness. He was looking for material reward instead of serving out of a heart of love toward his loving father. How did he miss the love of the father (vv. 31, 32)?

In what ways are you like the older son?

I'm so glad you answered those questions honestly. Only when we are truthful with God can our hearts be sensitive to his voice. Pray to God about your motives. Write your prayer here if you would like.

I believe God has hardwired women for relationship, so we have an inborn desire to be liked. This desire permeates our relationships, and it also haunts our relationship with God. Yes, we are beginning to understand the truth that God loves us and will never stop loving us. *But . . .* whispers the insecure voice in the depths of our inner being, *does God like me?* We can all list our irritating or undesirable traits. (Don't be fooled—it's the enemy on your shoulder telling you what to write.) And because of this list, we conclude that we are unlikable. Dear Princess Unaware, let's get in God's Word and hear from him on this matter.

Psalm 139 is loving assurance from God that we are constantly in his care and attention. We will study verses 13-16. In verse 13 David (the psalmist) says God created his *inmost being*. The meaning is "a kidney (as an essential organ)" and figuratively, "the mind (as the interior self)."[15] Insert those definitions into verse 13. How does it read?

Yes, God created your insides—your organs and how your body works, and he created your mind—who you are, how you think and feel, your very being. Remember from our study of Ephesians 1:1-9, we are chosen, forgiven, and accepted because it pleased God. "As for God, his way is perfect" (Psalm 18:30). God doesn't make mistakes. He not only designed me to be a tall, red-haired woman covered in freckles, but he made my outgoing personality. I am exactly the way God wants me.

From Psalm 139:13-16 list the phrases that show God's intentionality in your design and creation.

Describe yourself according to verse 14.

Write a line or two to God, expressing what you know "full well" about yourself.

✦ ✦ ✦ ✦ ✦ ✦ ✦ ✦ ✦ ✦ ✦

DAY TWO: The Princess Believes Her Father Is Faithful

Joshua was a normal guy, but he had a heart for God. He trained under Moses for years, doing the grunt work and watching God work in and through Moses in amazing ways. When it was time for the Israelites to go into the promised land, God chose Joshua to lead them. I can only imagine the pressure and fear Joshua felt. Joshua needed a word from God, and God spoke it to him. Read Joshua 1:1-9. How do we see God's faithfulness (vv. 5, 9)?

OK, you say, that's great for Joshua, but what about me? Turn to Hebrews 13:5. What does it say about God's faithfulness? Who is it talking about?

God is true to his Word. He was there for Joshua. He is there for us. Applying God's faithfulness to our lives is the hard part because when we do, we are called into action. Let's go back to the beginning of Moses' call from God. Read Exodus 3:1–4:17. Note how God gave Moses instruction with an assurance of who he is, his power, and faithfulness to Moses and Israel. Put a plus sign in your Bible next to each of those occurrences. Write down any that stand out to you.

Now note where Moses gave God excuse after excuse of why he was not the right person for this awesome mission. Put a minus sign next to those verses. Write down any of those that stand out to you.

Exodus 3:5 tells us Moses was standing on holy ground. With God speaking to Moses from the burning bush, Moses still did not want to accept his mission. Did he not believe God? The Bible doesn't say, but I think that Moses *did* believe God and that's why he didn't want to step out in faith.

In the longer passage, note what God told Moses regarding any obstacles he would face. Now note the verses in which Moses came up with his own obstacles. God told Moses he would have one obstacle—the king of Egypt would not let the Israelites go without a fight. Moses came up with three excuses:

✦ "What if the Israelites want to know your name?"
✦ "What if they don't believe me?"
✦ "I just can't speak well."

Think About It

What about you? What situation or adventure is God asking you to experience by trusting in his faithfulness?

What is the very next step God has shown you to do? Don't look ahead two or three steps and start fearfully coming up with obstacles like Moses did.

Use this space to commit to God that you will do the next step he has shown you.

Dear Princess Unaware, I know, believe me, *I know* that stepping out in faith with God is hard, scary work. But I can tell you that nothing is more rewarding than getting to the other side of the experience and saying, "What a thrilling ride with my faithful Father!"

✦ ✦ ✦ ✦ ✦ ✦ ✦ ✦ ✦ ✦ ✦

DAY THREE: The Princess Learns She Can Trust Her Father

Today we are going to talk about God's *sovereignty* and focus on how it affects our relationship with God. The question we want answered is, Can we trust God with our families and friends?

To answer this question, we must know God's motives toward us. (Very good! I heard you shout, "He loves us!") The term *providence* is not found in the Bible, but it can help us understand God's sovereignty. *Providence* "has been traditionally used to summarize God's ongoing relationship to his creation. . . . We may define God's providence as follows: God is continually involved with all created things in such a way that he (1) keeps them existing and maintaining the properties with which he created them; (2) cooperates with created things in every action, directing their distinctive properties to cause them to act as they do; and (3) directs them to fulfill his purposes."[16]

Let's get our brains in high gear and think this through. Reword each of the above points. Keep it simple and general. I know this is hard work, but it will be worth it.

Point 1

Point 2

Point 3

God's providence is always working on our behalf to keep creation operating the way he planned. God's providence "brings about various events in our lives."[17] God's providence guides our lives so we can live the rich lives he has for us. "Our words, our steps, our movements, our hearts, and our abilities are all from the Lord."[18] How does better understanding God's providence increase your trust in God?

Let's look at a couple of verses that will continue to build our confidence in God's best for us. Read Psalm 34:10. Are you seeking the Lord, or are you seeking only his blessings? How do you know?

Read Psalm 84:11. No one is truly blameless, but as you learned in the last chapter, if you are God's princess, you are blameless before him. Are you walking with God—trying to live each day as he directs you, not living in a sinful habit, keeping your relationship with him fresh? If no, what do you need to change?

If you are seeking the Lord and walking with him, yet you are going through hard times, how do you reconcile that?

The prophet Habakkuk understood and trusted in the sovereignty of God. Read Habakkuk 3:17-19. Then substitute the details of your difficult circumstances for the ones Habakkuk lists.

Make verses 18, 19 your prayer, your posture in the Lord. How do these verses change your perspective on the issues you just listed?

A dear friend's husband was in full-time ministry (which means she was too). They had a beautiful family and were surprised to discover another baby was on the way. Just a few weeks into the pregnancy, a sonogram revealed a severe problem with the child. The baby lived for only a few hours after she was born, before she went into the arms of Jesus. We grieved deeply with this family.

Why did this happen to them? These people were serving God with all they were and had. I don't know the answer; only God does. But through this difficult time, there was an outpouring of support for them. At the baby's memorial service, I looked through a scrapbook my friend had put together with e-mail after e-mail from people all over the world, encouraging them and being encouraged by them. My friend's life was watched closely, and even though she and her husband suffered deeply, they honored the Lord through it. Their lives spoke more than words ever could. I don't have answers to the whys of hard things in our lives. But God does. He is sovereign. I rest in that.

✦ ✦ ✦ ✦ ✦ ✦ ✦ ✦ ✦ ✦ ✦

DAY FOUR: The Princess Learns Her Father Listens

We women love to communicate—some more than others. And with that comes the need to be heard. Today we will look at four biblical truths that will lead us into closer communication and relationship with God.

Daniel is an excellent example of someone who had clear communication with God. Let's soak in Daniel 10:10-12. Daniel prayed and fasted for three weeks concerning a vision he had seen. When did God first hear Daniel's prayer?

The first truth is: your heavenly Father hears you as soon as you pray. Know that.

Daniel also prayed with earnestness. Daniel 2 recounts an impossible situation Daniel faced. The king had decreed that someone among the wise men of Babylon must tell him his dream and its meaning. Of course, that was impossible. Daniel and his friends gathered to pray to God for help. And that's the second truth: seek God. They asked "that they would desire mercies of the God of heaven concerning this secret; that Daniel and his fellows should not perish with the rest of the wise men of Babylon" (Daniel 2:18, *KJV*). *Desire* means "to seek or ask" and also "to gush over" or "swell out."[19] Daniel and his friends prayed as purely and sincerely as they could.

Describe a time when you poured it all out to the Lord.

How did that experience affect your relationship with him?

Jesus is always an excellent example for us. Hebrews 5:7 says (about Jesus' prayer in the Garden of Gethsemane right before he was arrested), "During the days of Jesus' life on earth, he offered up prayers and petitions with loud cries and tears to the one who could save him from death, and he was heard because of his reverent submission." Jesus' "loud cries and tears" prove he was earnest in his prayers. What does that tell us about our attitude and efforts in prayer?

Jesus and Daniel shared an attitude of humility in their prayer lives. The third thing that will lead you closer to God is humility. Let's go back to Daniel 10:12. What was the goal of Daniel's prayer? Do you have the same goal?

Let's look at Hebrews 5:7 one more time: "And he was heard because of his reverent submission." Jesus reverently submitted to his Father. He prayed with humility even though he is God. How does the principle of humility challenge the way you pray?

Read 2 Chronicles 34:14-27. List the responses of King Josiah to the reading of the law.

How did God respond to King Josiah's response?

King Josiah was authentically affected when he heard the Word of God read aloud. What is your usual reaction when reading or hearing the Word of God?

Have you thought of getting down on your face before God on your living room carpet, in awe of how he answered your prayer or in repentance of sin? The times I have done this have taken me to a deeper relationship with God. Have you stood and lifted your open hands to Heaven, giving God a loved one whose situation seems impossible? Reflect on how you respond to God and what you could do to "humble yourself before God."

The fourth truth we will look at today is that we can go boldly before God, which we also talked about in chapter 2. "So then, since we have a great High Priest who has entered heaven, Jesus the Son of God, let us hold firmly to what we believe. This High

Priest of ours understands our weaknesses, for he faced all of the same testings we do, yet he did not sin. So let us come boldly to the throne of our gracious God. There we will receive his mercy, and we will find grace to help us when we need it most" (Hebrews 4:14-16, *NLT*). Define *boldly* in your own words in the context of these verses.

In your praying, how will you reconcile the principle of boldness before God with the aspect of humility?

Looking Back

How did the week go? Did you soak in the love of God? Is that hard for you to comprehend and do? If yes, why? Which of the truths we discussed this week made the biggest impact on your life and why?

chapter four

Why Are Other Princesses So Difficult?

The Princess Identifies Common Relationship Mud Holes

The next morning Jessica put on a plain gingham traveling dress. Lady Penelope helped her carefully pack the blue silk dress and said, "Don't wear this one again till you arrive at the castle."

"Why not?" Jessica asked.

"You could encounter trials along the way," Lady Penelope said mysteriously.

Jessica had learned much from Lady Penelope about her new identity as a princess and about her Father. Now with Prince Cartier on his way to battle, Jessica was on her own again to finish her journey. Despite Lady Penelope's hint of warning, Jessica was filled with joy and confidence.

Nothing can stop me or slow me down. I am a princess!

Just ahead of her lay another forest. The foliage and underbrush was such a bright green, it almost glowed. The color of the flowers—reds and pinks and golds—was pure and clear. Princess Jessica picked up the pace. She couldn't wait to see the forest's beauty up close. Not far from the forest, she came upon a sign: "Forest of Amusements Ahead." Fun! And friends, no doubt! Jessica couldn't wait to meet some new friends. But hadn't her father said something about the Forest of Amusements when he sent her off on this journey? Surely a few hours wouldn't hurt . . .

Jessica entered the Forest of Amusements with high expectations. Immediately she came upon two girls her age enjoying a game, and she introduced herself to them. They were polite at first, but soon they turned from Jessica and started talking about her gingham dress.

"Surely that isn't the best she has," they snickered.

Oh no! I don't want to lose my only chance at having fun along the way, thought Jessica. "This is my traveling dress," she defended. "I have a nicer one in my satchel." *Now why did I say that? Lady Penelope warned me to save my other dress.*

"Really?" came one girl's sarcastic reply. "We can't understand how anyone would leave the house looking . . . *ahem* . . . less than presentable. What if some of our young gentlemen friends drop by?" she asked coyly. "Perhaps we should not like to be seen with peasants."

They giggled.

Jessica's thoughts went round and round. *Offer to put on the special dress. No, I'm to save it. But I want to impress these girls.* "I'll change into my blue silk," she offered enthusiastically.

"Please do change, and then we can go to my cottage for tea," said the other girl. "By the way, my name is Priscilla."

Princess Jessica ducked behind a large lilac bush and changed her dress, pushing away the nagging feeling that something was amiss.

Tea was pleasant enough. The talk was light and mostly about the others who stopped by the Forest of Amusements.

I wonder how the others will talk about me later? thought Jessica.

She noticed the sky turning red. "Thank you both for a lovely time, but I must be on my way."

Priscilla leaned over to give Jessica a good-bye hug, and in doing so, knocked over a teacup, splashing tea over the blue silk.

"Oops," Priscilla said sarcastically as the other girl started to giggle.

Jessica grabbed her satchel and ran out of the cottage. She struggled to keep her composure until she was a safe distance; then she broke down.

Why did I listen to those girls? I have nothing suitable to wear when I arrive at the castle. Why did I care what they thought?

Princess Jessica felt strong and confident because she knew she was the King's daughter, but what happened when she came upon a few peers? The same thing that happens to us when we get together with our peers—emotions and insecurities rule. My friend Jill has observed this in her relationships and ministry: "Our insecurities dominate everything. So many women let them rule their lives."

We begin this unhealthy behavior as children. We want to have friends and be part of the group, so we do what it takes to be accepted. We may dress and act the way the group dresses and acts, even if it means going against who we are. We may adopt the interests of the group, even though we are not interested or talented in those areas. We try to become someone we are not in order to be accepted by others. This creates insecurity. Of course it does—the same kind of insecurity an imposter acrobat would feel walking a tightrope.

We also operate on fallacies that we have absorbed, never examining them in the light of biblical truth. My daughter Kelsey took a communications class her freshman year at college. One night while helping her study, I quizzed her on communication fallacies. (A fallacy is a deception or a misleading or unsound argument.) As we went through the list, I got more and more excited (unlike my daughter, who was sick of this class). I began to understand how these fallacies were causing problems in my relationships and in other relationships that I had observed. For example, I wrongly believed it was up to me to make each of my relationships work—that if I tried harder, communicated better, and just hung in there, the relationship would improve and give me fulfillment. That is a fallacy.

No wonder we sink up to our eyeballs in the mud holes of comparison, people-pleaser peer pressure, criticism, and the I-don't-like-her-grating-personality muck. These mud holes pull us in and down like quicksand. The more we try to get out, the more we sink down. As I learned by watching *Man vs. Wild* (one of Kelsey's favorite shows), there is a right way to get out of quicksand and a wrong way. Most people try the wrong way and die.

Princess Jessica needed to learn to be confident in her relationships, and so do we. We do this by knowing God, knowing who we are in Christ, and having relationships based on truth. We have discussed the first two, so now let's dive into the third: healthy relationships. Let's talk about the right way to get out of four of the most common relationship mud holes women sink into—and the tools we need to avoid them in the first place.

The Comparison Mud Hole

Ooh, we women get sucked into this quicksand, and we barely put up a struggle to get out. We compare every area of our lives to the lives of other women:

Our appearance. Who has the best color on her hair? Who has the most desired body type—not too short, not too chubby, not too short waisted, not too flat, not too chesty? Who has the most stylish clothes? We are never pretty enough, stylish enough, or in good enough physical shape.

Our friendships. Who is better friends with whom? Who calls whom more often? *Why doesn't she ever call me? She is closer to her than to me.* Ugh.

Our kids. Oh yeah, this is a gem. Either our kids are superior or they never quite measure up to someone else's. *Why did her child make the team (or get a part in the play) and mine didn't?*

Our husbands. *Why can't my husband be as spiritual as the pastor? Why doesn't he bring me flowers for no particular reason? Why doesn't he feel my emotions and understand me deeply? Why isn't he the life of the party?* (We want our husbands to be a combination of Billy Graham, Dr. Phil, Jerry Seinfeld, Brad Pitt, and our best girlfriend—and to know exactly when we want them to play each role!)

Are you feeling silly? Do you see the pointlessness of comparing our lives to others'? The comparison game leads to self-absorbed introspection—thinking too often about ourselves. The trendy cliché "It's all about me!" manifests when we waste time comparing ourselves to others.

My friend Theresa says, "Comparison is death to friendships." The minute we start comparing, we build a barrier between us and the other person. Being a prisoner of this trap often tempts us to make a grocery list of our friend's perceived shortcomings and faults, or a list of every area in which we feel she surpasses us (and in our minds, looks down on us). As the list grows, so does our pity party—and with it, our dislike of our friend. Do you see how easily Satan uses these lists to put up barriers of inferiority, distrust, pride, and lies? We don't see the real person any longer—only our distorted perception of her. Not only do we distance ourselves from a good friend, we also fall for Satan's plan to isolate us from our sister in Christ.

Comparison breeds competition. Any competition ends up with winners and losers. How can we build healthy relationships when we see ourselves as better than our friends (victor) or inferior to them (loser)? Both positions are wrong and dangerous.

Feeling better than someone else is pride, and God hates pride. "God opposes the proud but gives grace to the humble" (1 Peter 5:5). Feeling inferior doesn't make you humble either. Beth Moore has written, "I'll never forget the first time

God exposed my periodic bouts of self-loathing as just another form of self-absorption. I was shocked, having thought all along that it was a sign of humility. Nothing like priding yourself in hating yourself. Beloved, let's let this one sink in deeply: constantly thinking little of ourselves is still thinking constantly of ourselves."[20]

I went through a time of comparing my ministry to other women's. I loved what I was doing, but I kept thinking I could also be doing what they were doing. One day God decisively spoke to me. He told me, "Your ministry is not theirs. Your ministry is unique—one I have given you." God impressed upon me that my ministry was his plan for me just as the other women's ministries were his plan for them.

Jesus dealt with a similar situation. John 21:15-23 records a conversation that took place during the forty days between Jesus' resurrection and ascension. Jesus restored Peter to ministry (after Peter had denied Jesus the night before his crucifixion). Then Jesus told Peter with "what kind of death he would glorify God" and challenged him, "Follow Me!" (v. 19, *NASB*). Peter was in the midst of this incredible, never-to-be-had-again-on-this-earth, one-on-one time with Jesus, and what did he do? He let his sinful human nature ruin it. Peter turned, saw John, and asked, in essence, "Hey, what about him?"

Peter, Peter, Peter! Why waste precious time with Jesus by comparing and being nosy about Jesus' plans for John? I love Jesus' shoot-from-the-hip response: "If I want him to remain until I come, what is that to you? You follow Me!" (v. 22, *NASB*).

Jesus has a plan for us. He is working that plan. At times he reveals to us part of that plan. The rest is trust and obey. Jesus' plan for us doesn't leave room for comparison. I love that.

The People-Pleaser-Peer-Pressure Mud Hole

This mud hole is the one Princess Jessica fell right into with the Forest of Amusements girls. She wanted to be part of their group. She felt insecure, so she offered to do something she shouldn't have in order to get their approval. But who needs their approval? As princesses of the King, we must realize that we have the only approval we will ever need—the approval of the King.

People pleasing looks innocent, but once we start sinking into it, we become obsessive. This trap is especially effective on Christians. Don't we all want everyone to like us? Isn't it one of the Ten Commandments—Thou shalt keep all people happy with you at all times? I mean, if someone is not happy with me because I don't meet expectations, isn't that my problem? No, this is one of the fallacies on which unhealthy relationships are based. Our happiness does not depend on the other person's liking us; and it is not our God-given responsibility to keep the other person happy with us at all times.

I love what Paul wrote about this: "It matters very little to me what you think of me, even less where I rank in popular opinion. I don't even rank myself. Comparisons in these matters are pointless. I'm not aware of anything that would disqualify me from being a good guide for you, but that doesn't mean much. The Master makes that judgment" (1 Corinthians 4:3, 4, *The Message*). The *NIV* says, "I care very little if I am judged by you." The word *judged* here means to "scrutinize," "investigate," "question, discern."[21] Paul didn't care that people were checking him out, even in a biblical way. He knew to whom he answered and who would ultimately make "that judgment." Whew! Feel the freedom in that. Soak in this maybe-new-to-you concept: it is not your mission on earth to keep everyone happy with you or to do what they say. They are not your boss.

Years ago I frequently fell for this trap. I know how insecure and miserable it made me feel. Now I hate to see other women suffering in the same way just because someone is not happy with them. Those other people are not God. We live to please God and none other.

Now when I am tempted to fall into this mud hole, I remember Jesus. The Gospels are full of examples of Jesus standing firm in truth when dealing with the Pharisees. Taking a stand against the Pharisees was a gutsy move in Jesus' day. The Pharisees were "the popular party. . . . They were extremely accurate and minute in all matters appertaining to the law of Moses."[22] The Pharisees said who was in and who was not. Yet Jesus boldly persevered in speaking the truth and not caring what they thought. He never walked away from one of their discussions thinking,

I hope I didn't make them mad. No way! Jesus spoke the truth in love—in a way they could hear and respond to if they chose.

Too often we go along with what we know is not right based on what God has called us to, just to keep the "popular party" happy with us. As in Jesus' day, sometimes the popular party is the bunch with whom we go to worship. Gene and I are currently going through a situation with one of our daughters. Our daughter's Christian friends stay busy with hanging out, youth group, hanging out after youth group, and did I mention more hanging out? These are good kids, and they are doing nothing wrong. However, Gene and I have decided to raise our girls with a more balanced approach to life. Our daughter is taking a summer class and working. If she fills every other available moment with her friends, she has no time to be part of our family, fulfill her home responsibilities, and grow her relationship with the Lord. That's when her life gets out of balance.

Some parents may say, "Hey, wish that was *our* only problem." And there's the rub. Our daughter's not doing anything wrong. The Christian kids are hanging out, so why shouldn't she? Because living this unbalanced life is not what's best for her. Because everyone else is, is not the right motive. We live to please God, not the popular party—no matter who they are.

The Criticism Trap

Wow. I struggle with this muck. With every personality and differing spiritual gifts comes the opportunity for various "entangling sins" (see Hebrews 12:1). My entangling sin is criticism. There, I've said it.

I am a people person, but I am equally a move-forward-let's-get-this-done person. The combination of the two (the sanguine and choleric personalities) gives me the passion that fuels the ministry God gave me—boldly sharing the truth of the Word with women and showing them that when they apply its truths, their lives will be transformed. I am mindful that there is much I don't know and much I don't even know I don't know. However, when I see a sister in Christ choosing to believe one of Satan's lies and wallowing in it—refusing to acknowledge the truth and move forward—I can become critical.

The word *criticism* doesn't appear often in any translations of the Bible, but its synonym *judging (judged, judgment)* does. Judging can take two forms. The first appears in Matthew 7:1, 2, where Jesus said, "Do not judge, or you too will be judged. For in the same way you judge others, you will be judged, and with the measure you use, it will be measured to you." Here *judge* means "to distinguish" or "decide." By implication it means "to try, condemn, punish . . . avenge . . . call in question."[23] We are not to judge, or we will face the same negative judging we are giving to others. The issue here is an attitude of supremacy, of believing we're in the position to judge others' weaknesses and sins.

The other kind of judging appears in 1 Corinthians 2:15, 16, where Paul wrote, "The spiritual man makes judgments about all things, but he himself is not subject to any man's judgment: 'For who has known the mind of the Lord that he may instruct him?' But we have the mind of Christ." Paul said that "the spiritual man" makes judgments, even about "all things."

But we're not supposed to judge, are we? Once again, the issue is in the attitude. The judging spoken of in Matthew 7 taps into our critical spirit—we can end up thinking we are better than others; whereas in 1 Corinthians 2, judgment refers to gathering information and being discerning. The word *discern* used in the context of judgment (as in 1 Kings 3:11) means "to hear intelligently (often with [implication] of attention, obedience, etc.)"[24] When we judge with discernment, there's no room for that awful attitude of supremacy that leads to criticism—putting ourselves above others and believing that we know better, behave better, and are more intelligent or more deserving.

Oswald Chambers's comments on Matthew 7:1, 2 spoke to me in a way I immediately could understand. He said, "The great characteristic of a saint is humility—Yes, all those things and other evils would have been manifested in me but for the grace of God, therefore I have no right to judge."[25] Hmm. Interesting perspective. Kinda hard to judge when you put it that way!

So when I see a sister in Christ making decisions or living in a way that goes against God's Word, I am biblically called to recognize it for what it is—sin. However, I am told by Jesus that I am not to judge her. I am not to bring down the gavel, declaring a verdict and sentence. I am not to look down on her. I am to realize that it easily could have been me. Then I am to *agape* love her and pray for her.

I confess that I have been judge and jury too many times. Would I want others judging or condemning me when I am the one sinning? It took only one time of being on the receiving end of condemnation to give me my fill—causing me to check myself and break this sinful habit. One of our daughters went through a season of making poor decisions, one after the other. At first I was shocked; then I learned to brace myself for whatever she would share with us next. In the midst of this, I needed to be prayed for and listened to. I did not need a lecture or a judgment on how she was not walking with the Lord. I had a handful of women whom I knew would not even consider judging me or my daughter but who listened and prayed. And the extra blessing to me was that some of these friends shared with me about their own times of poor decisions and how God had worked in their lives.

The I-Don't-Like-Her-Grating-Personality Muck

I am guilty of walking wide-eyed into this one. Some people we just like to dislike. Not very Christian, I know. And I know my personality is easy for some to dislike too. I'm not everyone's flavor. However, I don't want others to dislike me just because they don't like my personality. That's how Satan gets us.

God gave me an education in this some time ago. I was involved for a weekend with a small group of people (most of whom I did not previously know). We gathered for the first time, made our introductions, and sat down for dinner. Immediately, one of the women started guiding, even dominating, the conversation—and I could tell she was *that* personality. I braced myself for a long weekend. But in my hotel room that night, God had a talk with me. He showed me that this wasn't just an issue of my preference but a sin issue. I was choosing to dislike this woman because I didn't like the way God made her. I confessed my sin and repented, asking God to help me.

God is the perfect teacher. The next day he revealed this woman to me in a way I'd been unwilling to see the day before. Throughout the day she and I shared brief conversations as we had opportunity. She shared her struggles and weaknesses. I was shocked. She was vulnerable and gave credit to God for any good her ministry accomplished. I was humbled by God too. He had made her in his image and created her personality and ministry. It was only his business how he worked in and through her. How dare I put her on my "undesirable" list!

A friend explained to me how over the years God had shown her which personality types can cause her to walk wide-eyed into this quicksand. She noticed that each time she had a hurtful relationship, the other person involved had a specific personality type. I reflected on her insight and realized the same is true for me. By knowing this information about ourselves, we can better anticipate Satan's traps and know how to biblically proceed when we clash with another personality. We are wise to understand how God has made us—our personality type, spiritual gifts, and core fears—and then to apply the same knowledge to understanding others. Common names and characteristics for the four basic personality types are: sanguine (spontaneous, cheerful, life of the party); melancholy (thoughtful, faithful, moody); choleric (adventurous, confident, take-charge); and phlegmatic (patient, contented, laid-back).[26]

Months after my weekend with my grating-personality-so-I-don't-like-you friend, I came upon this quote from Beth Moore: "[God] calls us to love with insight. This is so important because our testy people and our foe both have something broken. If we will let Him, God can give us a heart of compassion and love for them that we did not think possible."[27] That is exactly what I experienced. I did not have to search long. During our second day together, my new friend shared with me her brokenness. As a result of my talking-to (as my mom used to say) from the Lord, my heart was ready to respond with a heart of compassion for her.

About now you might be ready to run from relationships, as Princess Jessica did, hoping the stain of poor decisions can be removed. But help is on the way. In chapter 5 we will discuss four biblical principles (love, friendship, forgiveness, and trust) that will ready us to have and nurture healthy relationships. I know this is hard work and many women are afraid to go here—but not you. You are a strong, confident princess!

Finding the Fabulous

We may think friendships are easy and should come naturally, but as we saw with Princess Jessica, all relationships are not friendships. Jesus will be our role model for doing relationships as God intended.

Looking Ahead

As you go about your week and your study, take note of how susceptible you are to the mud holes we are discussing. There will be a quiz!

✦ ✦ ✦ ✦ ✦ ✦ ✦ ✦ ✦ ✦ ✦

DAY ONE: The Comparison Trap

There are seven years between our oldest, Katie, and our youngest, Kerry; and five years between our middle child, Kelsey, and Kerry. Since the older two are . . . older, I expect them to act more maturely than their much younger sister. Duh! However, when they've been in tussles over sibling issues (with girls, that can be almost anything), the older two have reverted to acting as young as the youngest. To bring a moment of clarity, I often posed this deep question to Katie and Kelsey: "How old are you?" And then I answered for them: "You are eighteen and you are fifteen and your sister is ten. You two are acting like your sister. Act your age!"

Dear Princess Unaware, I must say to you also, "Act your age!" We are professional in our careers and sacrificial in caring for our families. Yet when it comes to relationships with other women, we sometimes revert to our junior high years. We size each other up constantly—comparing our tired wardrobe to our friends' trendy threads, comparing the size and interior design of our homes to other women's larger or more stylish homes, even comparing our spirituality (or our family's) to that of the people we sit with in Sunday school or church. Our comparisons may sound more Christian than when we were in junior high, but the bottom line is, we're still comparing ourselves to someone else. In what areas do you compare yourself to others? How do you come out, the winner or the loser?

Read Romans 15:7. What is your response?

Look at the verse again. Christ accepted you. In what specific ways does that help you accept yourself? Maybe this is a verse you want to include on an index card.

Let's dig into John 21:15-23. Imagine yourself in Peter's place in verses 15-19. Sure, it's not all easy stuff, but it is a rich conversation with the Lord. Describe a particularly sweet time of God's blessings to you or a precious time of fellowship with God.

How hard is it to stay in that communion with God before it is interrupted by thoughts of what others have or what God is doing in their lives?

Reread verse 19. When has Christ said to you, "Follow me!" but you have been too distracted to obey because you were looking at others?

Recall the times you have thought, *Lord, what about her?* (see v. 21). Check any of the following questions you have asked:

- ❏ *Why does* she *have an exciting, powerful career?*
- ❏ *Why does* she *have a perfect family?*
- ❏ *Why does* she *have so many friends?*
- ❏ *Why does* she *have so many opportunities?*

I have struggled with keeping my eyes on Christ and where he is taking me, as opposed to watching my sisters in Christ and where it appears he is taking them. Allow the Lord to speak to you through verse 22. What's he saying?

Dear Princess Unaware, if the Lord wants to use your sisters in a certain way or if he wants to bless them uniquely, then "what is that to you?" You must follow Jesus!

What honors God and draws us closer to him? The theme of Psalm 119 (all 176 verses!) is the psalmist's love for Scripture. Read verses 36, 37. In light of our discussion about comparison, what would you consider "selfish gain"?

What would you consider "worthless things"?

What does the psalmist say we should be thinking about?

The strong, confident princess wears her crown well, knowing whose she is and who she is. She trains her thoughts to go to her Father—thinking on his character and how much he loves her. That thought process leads to a full, satisfying life, because she is living as her Father planned, not chasing the garbage trail laid out by the enemy.

✦ ✦ ✦ ✦ ✦ ✦ ✦ ✦ ✦ ✦ ✦

DAY TWO: The People-Pleaser-Peer-Pressure Mud Hole

We all must guard against that peer pressure to fit in. If we don't wear our crowns well in all relationships, our insecurities kick in and we want more than anything to be accepted by a friend or the group. We may be tempted to spend more money than we have in order to keep up with the group. We may be tempted to trash-talk our husbands because other women do. We may be tempted to take on more ministry than we are called to—neglecting our families so we can keep our place in the group. Or we may be tempted to abandon our values and act in immoral ways because other friends we hang out with are doing it.

With the story of my daughter and the popular party of her friends in mind, describe a time that you let your life get out of balance just so you could stay in the favor of the popular party.

Think of a time when you gave in to peer pressure as an adult. What motive caused you to give in? What was your experience?

Not pleasant, I know. Don't condemn yourself, but see this for what it was—giving in when you knew it was not the right thing. Remember this and use it as resolve to be the strong, confident princess.

Now let's combine Scripture with that resolve for a plan for sure success. I love the book of Isaiah. It is so deep and rich. This prophecy is talking about Jesus, and that makes it all the more powerful: "For the Lord God helps Me, therefore, I am not disgraced; therefore, I have set My face like flint, and I know that I will not be ashamed. He who vindicates Me is near; who will contend with Me? Let us stand up to each other; who has a case against Me? Let him draw near to Me" (Isaiah 50:7, 8, *NASB*). Once again we have Jesus as our perfect example. These verses give us insight into Christ's thoughts and teach us how we are to respond to peer pressure.

I want us to delve into these verses so we don't miss a drop of their precious truth. Who helps you? Who do you most often turn to when you are in need of help? List them all.

Why are we not to feel disgraced?

What would it mean to "set [your] face like a flint"?

What thoughts come to mind when you read: "Let us stand up to each other"?

Share some specific ways you can stand up to the popular party with truth and graciousness.

Breathe in the refreshing breeze of that truth. Your heavenly Father, the King, helps you. There's no disgrace when you set your face like a flint—determined to do what the King has shown you. We can with graciousness and boldness resist peer pressure ("stand up to each other"), because we know who vindicates us. How will you respond differently the next time you feel peer pressure coming on?

The second part of this mud hole, people pleasing, is camouflaged in pseudo-Christian theology that says, "Thou shalt keep all people happy with you at all times." Do you believe it's your responsibility to obey this "command"? If yes, please find a collaborating Scripture reference and write it here. If no, how do your relationships and decisions reflect that?

Even Jesus did not keep everyone happy with him all the time. Look at John 7:1-9. What was the attitude of Jesus' brothers?

How do you think Jesus felt in response to their comments?

How have you felt when you've been misunderstood by those close to you?

How did Jesus respond to his brothers?

Jesus is always our perfect role model. He calmly spoke the truth in love to his brothers, even though his heart was hurting. He was being misunderstood, and they were not recognizing the Messiah. We can follow Jesus' example by realizing that everyone is not going to understand or support our choices. It is not our job to make them understand but to follow the Lord in obedience and entrust them to the Lord.

✦ ✦ ✦ ✦ ✦ ✦ ✦ ✦ ✦ ✦ ✦

DAY THREE: The Trap of Criticism

We think we are so smart when we adopt an attitude of "I see your sin." But Jesus has some stern words for us in Matthew 7. Let's look back at verses 1-5 and learn from our Teacher.

We have already discussed verse 1, "Do not judge, or you too will be judged." Verse 2 might make us a bit more uncomfortable: "For in the same way you judge others, you will be judged, and with the measure you use, it will be measured to you." Immediately, my measuring cups come to mind. Have I been generous and overflowing with grace to others? Or have I scantily measured out grace one fraction of a cupful at a time? When Gene makes coffee, he heaps the spoon till it overflows and then dumps one spoonful after another into the pot. He makes the best, richest, strongest coffee. I love it! I must confess I don't always heap God's grace on others that way. Do you? Tell the King about it here.

Read verses 3-5. If we are noticing a speck of sawdust in our sister's eye, are we missing the plank in our own? Oswald Chambers had something to say about this: "The reason we see hypocrisy and fraud and unreality in others is because they are all in our own hearts."[28] Ouch. Can we be honest with ourselves and the Lord here? Do you tend to be critical? If so, what is your MO?

❏ finding fault
❏ condemning others
❏ labeling others
❏ deciding what consequence others deserve

Be honest here. It's just you and the Lord, and he already knows anyway. What else would you like to add to the list?

James 4:11, 12 gives us a stern warning: "Brothers, do not slander one another. Anyone who speaks against his brother or judges him speaks against the law and judges it. . . . There is only one Lawgiver and Judge, the one who is able to save and destroy. But you—who are you to judge your neighbor?" These verses add another dimension to judging. The meaning of *judge* here is the same as in Matthew 7:1, 2. In your own words define *judging*.

The Ryrie Study Bible comments on these verses: "The person who judges his brother disobeys the law, thus putting himself above it and treating it with contempt."[29] Wow. Have you thought about judging others as putting yourself above the law? What thoughts come to your mind as you read this quote?

If we're supposed to be thinking Christians, how are we to think? Let's go back to 1 Corinthians 2:15, 16. These verses say we're to make "judgments about all things." What does *judgment* mean in theses verses?

We are to see the truth of a person or situation but not condemn. Think of a time you were judged or criticized whether or not the "judge and jury" had grounds. How did it feel?

How will remembering that experience help you in the future?

✦ ✦ ✦ ✦ ✦ ✦ ✦ ✦ ✦ ✦ ✦

DAY FOUR: The I-Don't-Like-Her-Grating-Personality Muck

This is an issue we all deal with. Let's examine it and formulate a plan for victory instead of falling into this muck at every social, professional, and spiritual gathering. Let's get real—we all have a specific personality type that grates on us. We need to understand that and admit it. Think about different people who grate on you, either presently or in the past. What are their personality traits?

Is there one personality type that keeps coming to mind?

Don't feel ashamed. (Don't forget—no doubt *you* drive someone else crazy too!) We are all wired with different preferences. God made us that way. And though he didn't create the other people to drive us crazy, he can use them to refine us.

Now that you know this information, you are ready to make a plan for victory. Let's reread Romans 15:7. I love the way the *Amplified Bible* puts it: "Welcome and receive [to your hearts] one another, then, even as Christ has welcomed and received you, for the glory of God." *Receive* here means "to take to oneself," to "admit (to friendship or hospitality)."[30]

Here Paul is teaching us to have an attitude of acceptance and a heart ready to receive our grating-personality friend. Here we are preparing our hearts with the love of God to see others the way God does—not judging, condemning, or criticizing. The attitude is one of acceptance. How can you agree with God to accept those with the personality type that grates on you, to prepare your heart to be endeared to these people?

Can you describe a time when you did this—and the blessing or victory you experienced as a result?

Accepting our Christian sisters, as well as our nonbelieving friends, is so important. We need a posture of heart that says to God, "Work in me, change me, and I will cooperate." Write a note to God, getting your heart ready for the work he wants to do in you.

According to Romans 15:7, Christ has already accepted us. Recently I spoke on this topic at a retreat. In response to a quiet-time assignment, one young woman shared the following: "I am the chosen daughter of Christ, a princess. I am loved and redeemed—freely given grace, forgiveness, belonging, hope, and salvation. I am *not* perfect. God knows that and actually designed me that way so that I would rely on him. I can start fresh at any moment simply by asking."[31]

Think About It

Does the idea of Christ accepting you with all your imperfections humble you a bit? Does it make you grateful? Do you feel the dark cloud of your critical spirit slipping away and being replaced by the glorious light of Christ? How so?

When we accept others we are glorifying God. Accepting each other is totally against our sinful human nature, so when we do accept others, it is only by God's power. How does this truth motivate you?

I am always motivated (OK, almost always) by the opportunity to catch Satan at his game. When we accept others as we have been accepted, and God is glorified, then we are beating Satan at his game. Way to go!

Looking Back

How did the week go? Which mud holes did you find yourself in most often? Were you surprised by how often you fell into them? Why or why not?

chapter five
Royal Relationships 101

The Princess Learns
How to Relate to Others God's Way

That wasn't princessy, Jessica chided herself as she hurried away from the forest. *Those girls certainly weren't friendly. What did I do wrong? I guess I should have listened to Father's warning to go around the Forest of Amusements.*

As the sky turned redder and redder, she remembered a language lesson in which she had learned that the word *amusement* meant "without thinking." Jessica thought on this. *Not thinking, just playing. How was I lured into their games?* But she knew how—she'd failed to consider her father's instruction. Jessica had done what she *felt* like doing, not what she *knew* was wise. She was wiser now. Amusements were fine—at the proper time. And it was great to have friends—if they were truly friends.

Princess Jessica hurried a safe distance away from the forest and found a place to camp. She saw the silhouette of the castle in the sunset, but the castle was still a day's journey away. Jessica started a fire, gathered pine needles, and spread her blanket on top of the needles to make a pallet. She realized she had not eaten all day. Lady Penelope had given her bread and cheese as she hugged her and sent her on her way. As Jessica rummaged through her satchel for the food, her fingers recognized the smooth leather cover of Father's book. She pulled it out.

Lady Penelope's parting words echoed in her head: *Wisdom comes from unexpected places. This book shall reveal to you in due time things you will need to know.* Jessica felt both fear and peace. She put more branches on the fire and sat down to read by its blaze.

✦ ✦ ✦ ✦ ✦ ✦ ✦ ✦ ✦ ✦ ✦

Jessica should have listened to her father's warning regarding the Forest of

Amusements. Our own Forest of Amusements can be enticing and fun, yet also a most dangerous place. We desperately crave relationships, but those relationships can cause us deep pain. We must know how to proceed the way God has instructed us and not just act without thinking.

You may be feeling tea-stained and used by your own version of the Forest of Amusements, but help is on the way. As Lady Penelope recommended, Jessica turned to Father's beloved book for help, and that's what we will do too. Let's look at four biblical principles for having and nurturing healthy relationships.

Love—Agape, That Is

My dear friend Lauren is one of the most loving people I know. If I had to name one person who personifies Jesus in this area of love, it would be Lauren. She finds the good in everyone. She shows by her expressions and tone of voice that she is glad to see you and wants the best for you. She never speaks badly about anyone. She gives affection, service, and warmth, expecting nothing in return—no strings attached. Lauren loves with agape love.

Agape love does not come naturally or easily, but with God we can be more like Jesus (1 Thessalonians 5:23, 24). Lauren shared her struggle with me: "We will always be trusting the Lord to help us with this."

In chapter 3 we talked about God's agape love for us as manifested in his benevolence and desire always to do what is best for us, even when we don't deserve it. Jesus commanded us to love each other as he loves us (John 13:34, 35). In *Following Christ* Joe Stowell gives an explanation of Christ's love: "Christ's kind of love doesn't require that we fully like everything about the people we are caring for. It does require that we are fully interested in their needs and that we respond to them, not necessarily because they deserve it, but because we are committed to following Christ and replicating His responses to people."[32]

Agape love cares about other people and shows kindness to them, not because they deserve it but because that is what agape love is. If we want to be like our Lord, know him better, and shine for him, we must love others with agape love—

because that is what Jesus did for us when we were the ones spitting in his face, denying him in our words and choices, and hammering the nails through his hands and feet (see Romans 5:8).

Agape love covers a lot of relationship mud and muck, doesn't it? Agape love obliterates our desire to criticize and compare and takes away our need to be a people pleaser or to give in to peer pressure; it allows us to see our sister in Christ—or any friend—for who she is. It keeps us from sinking neck deep in the grating-personality quicksand, because we see the person as God sees her. Remember the weekend when I responded unlovingly to my I-don't-like-your-grating-personality person? If I had started out operating in agape love, the weekend would have started out more fun, and I would have been spared a talking-to by God. I would have wanted this person to have a great weekend of blessing. I would have seen past what bothered me about her and, instead, would have seen all that God was doing through her and in her; and I would have been open to learn from her sooner. Had I operated in agape love at the outset, I would have been more blessed.

God loves us without expecting anything in return (1 John 4:9, 10; John 3:16; Luke 15:11-24). For several years I watched my dear friend Cynthia live out this aspect of agape love. A brain tumor slowly stole her young, vibrant husband from her and their four children. She insisted on being his primary caregiver, even at the end when no one would have blamed her for bringing in nursing care. She always honored him before everyone, especially their children. Through all this she did not receive his love in return. The man she had married, who adored her, laughed with her, and shared his life with her was gone. He was no longer capable of returning the love she was giving him.

God does what is best for us (Matthew 7:7-11); he does good to us (Psalm 145:8, 9). We show agape love to others by doing what is best for them. This may be as obvious as helping them with a project or giving biblical advice. A false understanding of agape love is that we must do for others whatever they ask; but that is not always agape love. Sometimes the help others ask for enables them to stay in their sin, so agape love must say no. That may not *look* like love, but love does not enable people to continue in their sinful, destructive ways.

One night we received a phone call from a relative, an over-the-road truck driver. A police officer had stopped him for a safety violation as he was driving through our state. When the officer ran a check on his driver's license, he discovered this man is what our state calls a deadbeat dad and put him in jail. Our relative called to request bail money. My husband said no. We had financially helped this man many times before, and he had not used the money for the needs of his children but for his vices. It was not in his best interest to give him money so he could continue in his sinful ways. His best interest was to face the consequences of his wrong choices. Sometimes God lets us face the consequences of our sin so we are motivated to turn from it and obey him. Love says, "I won't help you hurt yourself or others anymore. I still care about you and will pray for you. I will visit you in prison, but I won't help you get out."

Love wants what is best. The strong, confident princess wants the best for others and shows kindness and graciousness to all.

Exercising Care in Friendship

For many years I was not able to distinguish between friendship and loving with agape, but looking at the life of Jesus makes the difference clear. Jesus loves all people (Ephesians 5:2); yet while he walked on this earth, he was friends with only a few. We know from the Gospels that he had the twelve and from them he drew his inner circle—Peter, James, and John. Jesus poured his life into these twelve men. He trusted his inner circle with more intimate and important issues and events, especially the transfiguration (Mark 9:2-9) and his prayer in the Garden of Gethsemane (Matthew 26:36-46). He wanted their support and encouragement. He trusted them with one of his most difficult moments on earth.

Jesus also had a great friendship with Mary, Martha, and Lazarus. "Jesus loved Martha and her sister and Lazarus. [They were His dear friends, and He held them in loving esteem.]" (John 11:5, *AMP*). They hosted Jesus in their home (John 12:1, 2). I'm sure it was a place he could relax in their company and be refreshed from the demands of ministry.

Jesus chose these men and women to be his friends—people he would invest in, people who were moving forward with him in the mission God gave him, people who refreshed him, people he could laugh with.

Yes, among these precious ones Jesus drew into his bosom of friendship was Judas. But Jesus knew what Judas was all about. Jesus was not naive or in denial about Judas's character. We may have Judases among our friendships. Not everyone will love us. Some will want to do us harm, even as they are smiling at us. We need to proceed wisely regarding those we cannot trust.

We are to be alert and discerning. In Ephesians 5:15-17 Paul teaches us this principle: "Be very careful, then, how you live—not as unwise but as wise, making the most of every opportunity, because the days are evil. Therefore do not be foolish, but understand what the Lord's will is." We must be wise. Jesus did not let other people rule his life or harm him (John 7:1; 11:45-54; Matthew 12:14-16). Yes, Jesus was finally tortured and killed at the hands of his enemies, but only because he obediently submitted to his Father's timing and plan. Too many times we let others use us and abuse us, all in the name of Jesus. We let others plan our days, even our lives. Let's be wise to our Father's plan for us and be discerning as far as who we let into the interior of our lives.

Jesus also teaches us to love our enemies. "Love your enemies and pray for those who persecute you" (Matthew 5:44). The word *love* used here is *agapao*, which means to love "in a social or moral sense."[33] So Jesus is teaching us to love our enemies by doing good to them, praying for them, and giving to them when they are in need (Proverbs 25:21, 22). We are to want what is best for them, not what will harm them.

The strong, confident princess knows whose she is. She wisely gets to know others well before she calls them friend. She will have some good friends who are nonbelievers and some who are believers. For the sake of her spiritual life, she must develop some strong friendships with those who are going the same direction she is—growing in the Lord, speaking the truth in love, acting in trustworthy and selfless ways. I have said to a handful of Christian women, "You cannot hurt me. I know your heart. So anything hard you have to say to me, I know comes from a loving heart and is for my best." A true friend says a hard thing for your benefit, not to release the ugly hurt in herself. And a good Christian friend will be on the same page spiritually, so you are both pressing on to "take hold of that for which Christ Jesus took hold of [us]" (Philippians 3:12).

Jesus was that kind of friend. He loved his disciples, but sometimes he had to say hard things to them. One time "Jesus turned and said to Peter, 'Get behind me, Satan! You are a stumbling block to me; you do not have in mind the things of God, but the things of men'" (Matthew 16:23).

Forgiveness

The Lord's command to forgive others is a much misunderstood one. I believe that sincere believers—those who want to do what the Lord commands—many times assume that forgiveness equals reconciliation and trust. It does not. Much work needs to be done to construct the bridge from forgiveness to reconciliation to restored trust. First, let's look at forgiveness.

In Greek, one meaning of *forgive* is "to send forth," to "lay aside," to "put (send) away."[34] We are commanded to send away the transgression. We are to let go of the offense, not saying it is OK, but trusting the only just Judge with the consequences. "In fact, Jesus commands us to build into our prayers a request that God forgive us in the same way that we have forgiven others who have harmed us (in the same 'personal relationship' sense of 'forgive'—that is, not holding a grudge or cherishing bitterness against another person or harboring any desire to harm them)."[35]

Many times when our girls get in a tussle, one will try to be Judge Judy—delivering the verdict and the sentence. The "convicted" sister comes and tells me the "sentence" dealt to her by the not-so-honorable judge. I call Judge Judy into *my* chambers and ask, "Do you want to be in charge or do you want me to handle it? Because if you want me to deal with the situation, you need to quit being judge and jury." Of course, the offended sister wants my justice because she knows it has power, while any sentence she would try to impose will not have any effect on her sister.

The same is true in our tussles with our friends. The sentence we try to give our offender is powerless to affect her. Our responsibility is to let go of the offense and let God deal with her. If we don't, the offense is like a cactus that we carry around close to us; with even the slightest movement, we feel its painful prick. It's there every time we get in the car, sit down to read the Bible, lean over the baby's crib to lift him up, bend down to kiss our loved ones, and lie down to sleep.

Why do we do this? We are the ones suffering, not the offenders! Instead, we could forgive; we could give the hurt or offense to God. He is our avenger (Romans 12:19). He will deal with the situation. Have you ever seen a princess accessorize her royal look by carrying a huge bag of stinky garbage everywhere she goes? Never, and how ridiculous! Then why do we—princesses of the Most High King—carry our stinky bags of unforgiveness with us? Put that garbage of unforgiveness where it belongs—in our Father's landfill. He will deal with it.

This is not easy, and that's why we need to pray, asking God for his powerful Holy Spirit to work in us. Our responsibility is to position our hearts in a place ready to forgive. Forgiving in no way absolves the offender of her offense. But once we give the offense to God, it is his to deal with. He is the just judge, the Ancient of Days (Daniel 7:21, 22).

Once we have forgiven, we can love with agape love. As an act of our obedience to our Lord, we will pray for the other person and do good to her. Only the Holy Spirit can get our minds around this spiritual concept. Let's put ourselves humbly at the Lord's feet as we ask for his help and healing. The strong, confident princess knows and trusts her Lord. She has given this toxic load to him and is living her life to the full.

Reconciliation and Restored Trust

After forgiveness, reconciliation and then the rebuilding of trust may be possible.

Jesus said about reconciliation: "If you are presenting your offering at the altar, and there remember that your brother has something against you, leave your offering there before the altar and go; first be reconciled to your brother, and then come and present your offering" (Matthew 5:23, 24, *NASB*). Of course, two people must want reconciliation and be willing to work to restore the relationship. As with all correct Bible study, we need to take the Bible as a whole and not pull out a single verse without making sure our interpretation agrees with the rest of the Word. So let's also look at Romans 12:18: "If possible, so far as it depends on you, be at peace with all men" (*NASB*).

The key here is "if possible, so far as it depends on you." We are commanded by Jesus to have a spirit of reconciliation—an attitude that says, "Hey, I've forgiven you and I'm ready to work out our differences and deepen our relationship." Yet we know that we cannot change another person's mind or heart. If the other person does not want to forgive or work out the situation in a healthy, biblical way, we cannot make her, and we are not held responsible by the Lord for her response. God made this point through Jeremiah the prophet: "They dress the wound of my people as though it were not serious. 'Peace, peace,' they say, when there is no peace" (Jeremiah 8:11).

We cannot produce peace or keep peace (reconciliation) when it doesn't exist in the relationship. Yet when two people want reconciliation, they can have it. Two of my younger friends recently had a conversation regarding reconciling their relationship. From experience and biblical training, they had caught the essence of what it takes for a successful reconciliation.

Reconciliation begins with an honest confrontation over a sin issue or an issue that is an obstacle in the relationship. If you value your relationship, however, don't make an issue out of a preference or where your pride has been hurt. If we examine perceived offenses in this context, we may find that many are due to not getting our way or thinking we have been slighted. But Ecclesiastes 7:20-22 tells us, "There is not a righteous man on earth who does what is right and never sins. Do not pay attention to every word people say, or you may hear your servant cursing you—for you know in your heart that many times you yourself have cursed others." Let's give each other some room for error. That's called grace. "A man's wisdom gives him patience; it is to his glory to overlook an offense" (Proverbs 19:11).

The best condition for reconciliation is an open, safe, loving, and committed friendship. However, if the relationship is not such a friendship, that doesn't mean that reconciliation cannot proceed. An attempt at reconciliation may be the next step to making this a safe, loving friendship.

In every attempt at reconciliation, a few basics apply:

+ Pray for a gentle, humble attitude.
+ Keep it simple and to the point. Do not drench the conversation in drama and emotion (Ephesians 4:15).
+ Keep to the facts, not perceived offenses or hurts (Ephesians 4:15 again).
+ Agree not to dredge up every offense from the past. If either party starts dumping, the other person needs to stop her or walk away from the conversation. It's just not allowed.

Remember, confrontation is not to make the other person feel your pain but to get the offense out in the open with the air cleared and both parties committed to moving ahead in a healthy fashion.

My friend Elizabeth came to me to discuss a problem, asking for advice about what to do next. Elizabeth had a strong, growing relationship with a friend, but then a situation occurred that caused Elizabeth to back away and not trust her friend. What was the right thing to do? We discussed this at length. Because it was an issue of trust and this friendship held such promise, Elizabeth decided to confront her friend in love. She followed the guidelines listed above. The result was fabulous. Because Elizabeth did not assign blame or use emotional manipulation, her friend immediately confessed her part in the offense and apologized, and the two were reconciled. I'm sure the Lord was smiling.

Every situation won't turn out this way. I have been part of a few that have not. The risk of being hurt again has to be faced.

If reconciliation is successful, you are ready to rebuild trust. *Trust* is defined as "assured reliance on the character, ability, strength, or truth of someone or something."[36] Rebuilding trust is a process, and it will take time.

If the offense was caused by a pattern of sin, give the person room to turn from her sin and start a faithful walk with the Lord before you welcome her back into the bosom of friendship. If the offense was caused by a lack of character, then patiently give her a chance to change. For example, if a friend has trouble being confidential, don't immediately start taking her into your confidence again, but pay attention over time to what she shares about others. If she tells you what others have told her in confidence, she will talk with others about what you have told her too, even if it's only with the friends she "trusts." If you see a real change in her, then try her with a piece of information that isn't too delicate. If it comes back to you, you will know she can't be trusted yet. God does this with us. He gives us small amounts of responsibility to see if we are trustworthy, and when we prove that we are, he gives us more (Matthew 25:14-30).

As we have examined these four principles of relationships—love, friendship, forgiveness, and trust—are you getting a clearer picture of how Jesus did healthy relationships and what he asks of us? The strong, confident princess knows what her responsibility is in relationships. She does well what the Lord commands and leaves the results to him.

Finding the Fabulous

I am especially passionate about the truths in this chapter because I have observed very few Christian women doing relationships well. Many mistakenly believe they cannot be honest about their thoughts or speak the truth in love, for fear of being misunderstood or offending someone. Some women go the opposite way and try to control and manipulate to secure relationships on their terms.

Neither of these approaches to relationships is based on the example of our Savior or his teachings. By learning the four principles in this chapter and incorporating them into our lives, we will be well on our way not only to healthy relationships but to success in other areas of our lives as well. Let's dig into the Word.

Looking Ahead

This week we want to study how Jesus did relationships and allow the Holy Spirit to show us any fallacies we may be operating under. Be alert and ready to share these on Day Four.

✦ ✦ ✦ ✦ ✦ ✦ ✦ ✦ ✦ ✦ ✦

DAY ONE: Love—Agape, That Is

The Greek language has three words for *love*. Our discussion will be focused on *agape*, which we've already seen is defined as benevolence, the desire to do what is best for someone else. It is agape love that Jesus told us to have for each other in John 15:17.

After reading that verse, what is your first impression of what Christ is telling us to do?

Jesus is not telling us to like the other person. He is telling us to love her with agape love. Read Matthew 7:7-12 and Psalm 145:8, 9. What stands out to you in those passages?

Agape love is seen in action; it's not a warm fuzzy. Agape love is what we do when we are truly followers of Christ. We are to show agape love to everyone, even those who are not in our e-mail address books. What would agape love look like in your life? What specific actions or words of encouragement/kindness would show agape love to each of these?

your family

your coworkers

your church family

the clerks at your grocery store, dry cleaners, and bank

OK, if you skipped that section, go back and think. How would Jesus show agape love—kindness, blessing, and benevolence—to the people in your life? This exercise is important for starting to see how Jesus did life on earth, so that we can be more like him—and truly the princesses that we are.

I was a Princess Diana fan, not because of her glamour, beauty, and position but because in her role she showed how royalty loves others with agape love. The "people's princess," Diana never forgot where she came from or the regular folks. Using her place of privilege to help those who couldn't help themselves, she was equally gracious and loving whether she cuddled an HIV-infected child or was shaking the hand of a world leader.

We are royalty. Our position as princesses of the King gives us the strength, power, and resources to agape love others. Think of your grating-personality person. With the information you know about her (circumstances, struggles, service, job, family, etc.), how could you show her agape love in the next month?

Now do it. Step out of your prison of prejudice and obey the Lord. I will do it; join me. The beauty of agape love is that when we love each other this way, the body of Christ shines for the world to see. It brings honor to God.

Agape love may mean backing off and letting God work in someone through her difficult circumstances. Let's take a look at how Jesus handled this type of situation. Read Matthew 19:16-23. How did Jesus love this man with agape love?

How do you think Jesus felt watching this man walk off toward an eternity without him?

We too can do everything as Jesus did—be kind, truthful, loving, and helpful—but for some people that won't be enough; nothing will be enough. Jesus let this man go and think over his decision. Who knows?—maybe he came to Christ later. But don't miss this point: Jesus did not try to fix this man. He showed him the way, but the man had to choose.

We women tend to be rescuers. I have the passionate (but also false) idea that if I can just get someone to know and understand the truth, she will make the right decision. That is a fallacy. God has given each of us our own free will to choose. But either we don't understand that or we refuse to accept it. As a result we cause more stress and trouble by trying to rescue our adult children, husbands, extended family, friends, or any stray puppy that comes our way. (OK, maybe the stray puppy is a little exaggerated, but you get my point!)

Who have you tried to rescue? Were you successful?

Dear Princess Unaware, I know the passion, compassion, and frustration you feel over the person or people you just listed. However, the truth is that only the Lord can change their hearts. Look into the Gospels and you will see that Jesus did not make everyone accept him as Savior, nor did he right every wrong; he did the mission God sent him to do (John 8:28-30).

Think About It

I know this is a deep and sticky issue. Prayerfully consider it, and don't hesitate to seek advice from a mature Christian or get professional Christian counsel. Think about someone you consistently try to help, whether with finances, counseling, employment, or some other way. What type of agape love does she need from you?

No matter how well you love with agape love in this difficult situation, you still may be considered the wicked witch. It just comes with the territory. But the strong, confident princess lets her Father's agape love live through her. She knows he will give her what she needs to love others as Christ did.

+ + + + + + + + + + +

DAY TWO: Exercising Care in Friendship

I'll let you start this part. List the good qualities or characteristics you expect in a good friend. This is not a trick question but a vital part of today's study. (Keep the list in mind as we proceed.)

Our friends can be good for us, or they can be a source of temptation, pain, and frustration. When we call someone friend, we are letting her closer to us—giving her more access to know more about us. We cannot trust everyone with that information. Look again at the characteristics you listed above. We need friends who are moving ahead with the Lord, who refresh us, who can be trusted. If we can laugh with them too, all the better!

Now make a list of your relationships. Who do you do life with? This may be women at your job, your kids' friends' moms, a friend miles away that you e-mail daily. Who do you hang out with, have coffee or lunch with? Who goes shopping with you when you *must* have a new dress? Who do you pour into and who pours into you?

Look back at your first list of friend qualities. Now look at your list of friends and relationships. Make a new list, matching the names of friends with qualities.

How does this help you decide which friends you will hang out with, pour yourself into, and allow to pour into you?

A discussion on friendships will almost always bring to mind a person who portrayed herself as a friend but through time and events was revealed as an enemy. This person wanted to harm you—maybe with rumors, lies, or innuendos or by sabotaging your project, stealing your commendation, or making life difficult. Jesus had enemies, and if you are walking with the Lord and trying to live as the princess you are, you will have enemies too.

Reread Matthew 5:43-48. What does Jesus tell us to do?

Most of us need repetition to really get a lesson to stick. Define *agape love* again.

Do you have an enemy? Write her first initial here: _____. How could you show her agape love in a way that is not dangerous to you?

Many times the only way we can love someone who wants to harm us is to pray for her (because it is not safe or wise to draw her close) and not do her harm—we won't gossip about her, for example.

One characteristic that our Father desires his princesses to acquire is discernment. God wants us to know what is from him and what is not. Read John 10:22-40. In case your Bible doesn't give helpful footnotes, the holiday is the Feast of Dedication, or

Hanukkah, which begins in late December and is celebrated for eight days. What was going on in verses 22-30?

Jesus had made the Jews furious by claiming to be God. In verses 31, 39, what did the Jews want to do to Jesus?

How did Jesus respond?

Jesus somehow freed himself from their grasp—from their intent to harm him. He knew God's plan for him, and this was not it. Let's do some life application here. God has a plan for our lives—a unique, loving plan. So why do we allow others to "grasp" us, to do with us according to *their* plans? Why aren't we following Christ's example and being discerning—checking with God to see what's what? If we ask God, he will show us what is part of his plan for us and what or whom we need to be careful around (James 1:5; Proverbs 2:1-6).

Once we know someone is a red-flag person for us, we need to carefully back away and stay sensitive to the Lord's leading. When God gave me the red-flag alert, I could not ignore the firm impression that accompanied it—*STOP. Do not go near her.* I did not understand for a long time. Months later God slowly revealed to me the harm this woman was trying to do to my reputation as a child of God. I obeyed God and he protected me.

Remember, not every person will love you. The religious leaders of Jesus' day had access to the truth but weren't living it. He called them a "brood of vipers" (Matthew 3:7). Yes, Jesus loved them and died for them, but he knew they intended to harm him and keep him from his Father's plan for his life.

The strong, confident princess knows two important truths regarding friendships:

✦ Friends do not define her or give her worth. She knows whose she is and who she is.

✦ The princess carefully discerns character, looking for quality friendships. She has learned to wait for and nurture a few good relationships rather than pour time and energy into many shallow or even harmful relationships.

One More Thing

I know that not everyone has friends, good or otherwise. I have gone through periods of not having friends and varying degrees of friends. This is a hot topic for women because many, many of us struggle with isolation and loneliness. Please don't be down on yourself if you are going through this. Take it to the Lord. Let him guide and heal you.

✦ ✦ ✦ ✦ ✦ ✦ ✦ ✦ ✦ ✦ ✦

DAY THREE: Forgiveness

Healthy, growing relationships will require forgiveness from both parties from time to time. Define *forgiveness* in your own words.

Describe a time you decided to be Judge Judy. Don't get ugly about it; just give a few details.

How did your attempt at being judge and jury turn out? Were you pleased with your decision and the result?

What will you do the next time you are tempted to be judge and jury?

Read Ephesians 4:32, Colossians 3:13, and Matthew 6:14. Princess Unaware, if you are accessorizing your royal look with a load of garbage right now, how do you think your Father feels about that?

Matthew 6:14 comes at the end of the prayer guide Jesus taught the disciples. What does Jesus say will happen if we forgive others?

A note in *The Ryrie Study Bible* clarifies this verse: "Forgiveness with the Father depends on forgiveness among the members of the family of God. This is the forgiveness that affects fellowship within the family of God, not the forgiveness that leads to salvation."[37]

This is a big deal. What do you think Christ is telling us here in regard to holding resentment, bitterness, or a grudge?

We are to forgive the offenses of others. This can only be done by the power of the Holy Spirit.

Jesus teaches more about forgiveness in Matthew 18:21-35. Read this as if you have never read the parable before. Allow yourself to feel the indignation of the situation. How could this pathetic servant be given so much—forgiveness of his debt and deliverance of his family and his life—and then go to his fellow servant, his equal in station, and make demands on him that he himself had been forgiven? What happened to the unmerciful servant (vv. 32-34)?

Read verse 34 carefully. We too will be tortured in some way in our unforgiveness. I'm sure we have all witnessed the destruction of a life because the person allowed unforgiveness and bitterness to take root. Please don't let this be you. No offense is worth surrendering your life to unforgiveness, because then you are allowing the offender to continue to hurt you. God has made provision for this hurt done to you. His Holy Spirit will help you forgive and will heal you. Right now, will you ask God to help you put your heart in a position to forgive—to give the garbage to him to deal with—and then ask him to help you forgive and move on in your life as the strong, confident princess?

This may need to be a process, not a one-time-fix-all project. And that is fine. Just be sure that every time this offense comes to mind, you immediately hand it right back to God. Don't dwell on it even for a second. Then have a verse ready to think on. Let God give you one. I love Isaiah 43:1: "Fear not, for I have redeemed you; I have summoned you by name; you are mine." After that penetrates your heart, you might want to go on to verses 2, 3: "When you pass through the waters, I will be with you; and when you pass through the rivers, they will not sweep over you. When you walk through the fire, you will not be burned; the flames will not set you ablaze. For I am the LORD, your God, the Holy One of Israel, your Savior."

After you forgive someone, you are free to love her with agape love. Prayer is a perfect way to start. Job, at the end of his ordeal, showed us a great example of forgiveness. He prayed for his friends: "After Job had prayed for his friends, the LORD made him prosperous again and gave him twice as much as he had before" (Job 42:10). By praying for those who hurt him, Job put himself in a posture to be blessed by God.

Recently God took me to this verse and challenged me to pray for friends who had hurt me. I had forgiven them, but now God wanted me to pray for them. I wrote their names in my prayer journal. Now I often pray for them—for blessing, for God to work in them. I know it sounds crazy. It's not the way the world does life, but it's the way God wants us to do life. Have you forgiven someone this week? How can you begin to pray for her?

✦ ✦ ✦ ✦ ✦ ✦ ✦ ✦ ✦ ✦ ✦

DAY FOUR: Reconciliation and Restored Trust

Forgiveness is something we can do no matter how the other person proceeds. But reconciliation and restored trust require two people. Read Matthew 5:23, 24 and

Romans 12:18. How do you understand these verses as instructions for trying to reconcile a relationship?

Reconciliation takes two people with humble, teachable attitudes working toward the common goal. As we are commanded to have a forgiving spirit, in these verses we are commanded to have a spirit of reconciliation—ready and willing to reunite.

Ephesians 4:1-16 explains God's desire for us to live in unity with other believers. Verse 1 provides our personal goal. What is that?

Verse 2 gives us our attitude. Describe it.

Verse 3 gives our instruction in relationships. Compare it with Romans 12:18.

Verses 4-6 give us our goal for living in the body of Christ. What is it and why is it important?

How are we to prepare for this goal (vv. 11-13)?

What happens when we are growing in the Lord and are becoming mature (vv. 14-16)?

Whew! What a spiritual workout! Good job. When we are following this plan of God for his people, everything comes together. We have a humble attitude (no more "It's all about me!"); we are patient with each other; we try to keep true, godly unity; we are using our gifts to benefit the body; we are growing and maturing; we will speak the truth in love and we will hear it in love; and we will become a united, healthy body of Christ.

Read Matthew 25:14-30. This parable talks about God trusting us with a little to see if we can handle more. How does the lesson in this parable apply to building trust in relationships?

Give an example of how you will proceed with this biblical principle.

 Looking Back

How did the week go? What fallacies about the way to do relationships did you discover? What biblical principles address those fallacies?

How have you been encouraged or challenged to develop healthy relationships?

Which of the biblical principles was most challenging? the most encouraging? How will these principles change the way you wear your crown?

I love learning about doing healthy relationships from my Savior, who lived on this same earth I live on with all kinds of people and situations. How are you allowing him to shape you a bit more into the strong, confident princess you are?

chapter six

Living Your Royal Dream

The Princess Discovers
Her Father's Plan for Her

After a long day of traveling, Princess Jessica approached the castle and walled village. She joined the throng of villagers crossing the drawbridge and entering the courtyard for the monthly market day. Small cottages and shops lined the wall that surrounded the courtyard and castle. Jesters entertained the crowds, and knights walked the streets to keep the masses under control. Villagers bartered. Mothers tended their children.

What a lovely place to live! thought Jessica. She ventured to ask one of the knights, "How do I gain entrance to the castle?"

His expression betrayed his surprise. Villagers took notice and gathered around. They began to crowd Jessica. One pointed to her medallion. The knight she was talking to summoned other knights, who surrounded her and whisked her into the castle.

Ladies-in-waiting descended on Jessica and bustled around her. "We've been expecting you!" said one. "Your family is on their way to the throne room. We will have you ready to meet them shortly."

Soon Jessica walked up the long aisle of the throne room, bowing deeply before the King, who was arrayed in the most magnificent robe and crown she'd ever seen.

"Child, arise. You do not need to bow." Her Father's voice was firm yet loving. "You are royalty. You are part of our family."

But Jessica *wanted* to bow. The King had the kindest smile and the brightest eyes . . .

Her sisters surrounded her with a chorus of cheers. The King gently diverted them to their royal duties, saying, "You will have a lifetime to get acquainted."

"Princess . . . Jessica . . ." the King said slowly, savoring the sound of her name. "How long I have waited to say those words. I wish to divulge to you why I sent you away at such a young age." He reached for her hand and enveloped it in his. "Our kingdom was at war. Since you are the youngest daughter, I deemed it best to send you away to the countryside. I chose a family I knew would cherish you and raise you according to my instructions. Though you didn't see me, Princess Jessica, I always cared for you—with provisions for your family, with knights posted along the roads, with falcons watching from the sky for predators—"

"Like Pit Weasels!" she exclaimed.

"Yes," he smiled knowingly.

They continued their conversation late into the evening. With delight dancing in his eyes, the King finally shared with Jessica the glorious plan that had been awaiting her all her life, a plan full of adventure and purpose.

Princess Jessica finally knows who she is and who her Father is. Now she is ready for the exciting phase of her life; the King has specific plans for her. The King has specific plans for you too. God has a call on your life. "I urge you to live a life worthy of the calling you have received," Paul wrote (Ephesians 4:1). In God's royal family each person has a special purpose and job—something you were uniquely designed to do, something that fulfills you and stretches you and accomplishes God's purpose through you.

Your past, your family of origin, your current situation . . . it doesn't matter if they're less than ideal. "God's gifts and his call are irrevocable" (Romans 11:29). If you have accepted Jesus Christ, God's Son, as your Savior, then you are God's child and he has a plan for you. He is waiting for you to get on board and live it.

I remember when the Lord began to stir me with a hint of his vision for me. At first I didn't believe it or acknowledge it. I thought my life would continue fairly uneventfully. I was a stay-at-home mom with two daughters, doing my best to be frugal and make the best life I could for Gene and the girls. I loved it and I still do. After the Lord they are my greatest delight and highest priority. But God was creating a desire in me, an itch, a stirring for something else. It was not to replace them, but it was to fulfill this other part of me that had lain dormant for so long.

God's plan for you existed before the creation of the universe. Ephesians 2:10 says, "We are God's workmanship, created in Christ Jesus to do good works, which God prepared in advance for us to do." I love that. God has prepared a special plan for me. It must be fabulous, because God doesn't do anything partway. And I was made in the specific fashion that makes me the perfect person for the works he planned for me. My personality, talents, abilities, and interests were made to do the things God stirs me to do. Yes, I can do other things, but I am most effective and living God's plan for me when I am doing the things he created me to do.

The dream God put in you is big. I'm not talking rich-and-famous big. I am saying this dream will be bigger than you, bigger than you dare to imagine. You will need God to accomplish it. Take a look at the people in the Bible whom God chose to use. We assign glamour to them because of the amazing works God did through them, but most of them were regular folks who were fearful when God told them what he had planned for them. Most were ordinary people going about their daily lives when God tapped them on the shoulder and said, "How about an exciting adventure with me?" These were people who didn't have enough faith, who slipped and sinned, who denied Christ, who fought with other believers, who wanted glory for themselves. But God enabled them to do their tasks from him well and successfully. He gave them what they needed to do the mission.

Mary, the mother of Jesus, comes to mind. Who in the world is prepared to raise the Son of God? Certainly not a young, unmarried teenager with no prior parenting experience. Mary knew she wasn't prepared, but she knew she was called by God. So she accepted her calling from God and trusted him for what she needed. God was faithful to her, and she faithfully completed her big mission from God.

The same elements will go into your story when it is told years from now. The mission was big—too big for you. You did not have what it took to complete it. How could you possibly succeed at this unattainable mission? But you chose to pursue it and succeeded the same way the heroes in the Bible did—by perseverance, focus, faith, trust, obedience—by walking closer with God than you imagined possible.

Understanding God's Plan for You

God's plan for you is not something you dream up as you sit with a cup of coffee and try to think deep thoughts. It doesn't come from you; it comes from God.

Discover Your Dream

You get it every once in a while—that small nudge or urge to do something to make a difference. Then you go through your list of reasons why you can't or why you wouldn't succeed, and your "logical thinking" squelches the dream. But not for long. The nudge becomes more like a push, and the push is almost strong enough to get you out of your comfy chair. Again your superior reasoning skills kick in: You have responsibilities. What will your friends say? You have never done this type of thing, and you are clueless about what to do next. The urge is squelched again. But this time it escapes to the front of your brain, and now you can't quite shake it. You find yourself thinking about this idea when you least expect to—driving home, packing lunches, in the shower (my best ideas come in the shower), weeding the garden. Now you are becoming restless because this dream is stirring your soul and you don't know what to do about it.

What dream or vision or mission has God made you to do? What passion, desire, or unmet need is stirring in you right now? If you could clear your schedule of everything but family and job (and your current job may become optional), what would you throw yourself into that would make a difference for the kingdom? What are you passionate about? The homeless community? Single moms? Post-abortion women? Children?—maybe inner-city kids, maybe the kids in your church who are not being taught basic doctrine and why it matters to them . . .

Some dreams wear secular clothing, and we might not recognize them as being from God. After I led a retreat session on discovering and living your dream, a young doctor came to talk with me. She was fascinated with what she'd discovered about her career: "So that's why it's so fun!" She was thrilled to realize that her profession—a pediatrician—was the calling God had for her. She was already doing it and loving it.

So what has God been stirring your heart with? Think about it. And when God reveals it to you, acknowledge it. No more squelching.

Discover Your Gifts

Finding your mission is only the first step. Have you discovered which spiritual gifts God has given to you? A spiritual gift is from the Holy Spirit. You have at least one. The Greek words for *spiritual gift* mean "supernatural" and "a (spiritual) endowment."[38] "A spiritual gift is any ability that is empowered by the Holy Spirit and used in any ministry of the church."[39] The spiritual gifts are listed in 1 Corinthians 12:7-10, 28; Ephesians 4:11; and Romans 12:6-8. A study of spiritual gifts is easily a book of its own, but we'll look at some in this chapter to get the idea.

If you do not know what your gift or gifts are, I urge you to pursue discovering them.[40] Here, from *Maximizing Your Effectiveness*, are definitions of a few spiritual gifts that are most easily recognized.[41] Please remember that each of these gifts is a God-given ability:

+ Administration. The "ability to manage or order the affairs of a church or parachurch organization."
+ Evangelism. "The ability to communicate clearly the gospel of Jesus Christ . . . to unbelievers individually or in a group context with the result that people respond and accept Christ."
+ Encouragement (or exhortation). "Involves encouraging, consoling, and when necessary confronting and admonishing others so they are benefited spiritually in their walk with Christ."
+ Faith. "The ability to envision what needs to be done and to trust God to accomplish it even though it seems impossible to most people."
+ Giving. "The ability to give eagerly, wisely, generously, and sacrificially to others."
+ Helps/Service. "The capacity to recognize and provide assistance in meeting practical needs, thus making life a little easier for others."
+ Teaching. The "ability to understand and communicate biblical truth."

We are told to use our gifts and not to let them be wasted. "A spiritual gift is given to each of us so we can help each other" (1 Corinthians 12:7, *NLT*). When we use our spiritual gifts, we are helping other believers and doing our part in the body of Christ. "God has given each of you a gift from his great variety of spiritual gifts. Use them well to serve one another" (1 Peter 4:10, *NLT*). We are blessed when we use our gifts, but as I wrote earlier, God doesn't bring us into his family so we can be waited on. We each have a role in the family. Serving in our area of spiritual gifts is fulfilling that role. We don't have to wonder any longer why God put us on the earth. Now we know.

In 2 Timothy 1:6 Paul urges Timothy to "fan into flame the gift of God." As with every other skill in life, the more we do it, the better we become at it. That is why it is important to take the opportunities to serve in our area of giftedness. When we say yes, instead, to all the other opportunities presented to us, we are diverted away from what God made us to do—and we end up doing what someone else was made to do. Think about that the next time you are tempted to say yes because it's easier than saying no thanks.

Paul also challenges us to boldly and purposefully develop and use our gifts. "God did not give us a spirit of timidity, but a spirit of power, of love and of self-discipline" (2 Timothy 1:7). No one in the family of God can play the poor-untalented-me card. You have one or more gifts. Discover them. Look for opportunities to use them. They are from God, and the Holy Spirit is working through you and in you, so be bold and confident in your service. This is how the strong, confident princess lives.

What Are Your Talents?

Our talents are different from our spiritual gifts. Talents are natural abilities. We all know people who seem to be a natural at what they do; that's because they are using abilities God gave them before they were born.

My daughters have musical talent; I do not. I have no rhythm. My fingers were never able to bring life to the piano keys. I tried to sing in my high school choir because my best friend coaxed me into it. It was a frustrating experience. But I have had a narrative running through my head for as long as I can remember, as if I were practicing a presentation of my day or my convictions.

Our talents will need training and practice, but the necessary resource is in us.

Are You Ready?

Once you put together your passion, your spiritual gifts, and your talents, you have a better understanding of what God has planned for you. My passion is for women to know God's truth and let it affect their lives. My gifts are teaching, exhortation, and faith. When I put my passion with my spiritual gifts and added my God-given talent to write and communicate, I was able to identify and act on the stirring God put in me years ago. Today I am an author and speaker who passionately shares God's truth with women, helping them apply it to their lives.

But understanding what you've been called to do and being ready to do it are not the same. Once I acknowledged what God put on my heart to do (and it took years), I thought I was ready to start immediately and that God would bring ministry opportunities one after the other to my door. I was wrong. God had quite a bit of work to do in me before he and I could begin, and I am still a lump of clay that he is working on. God knows what you need to start your calling. Cooperate with him.

Maybe you identify with a woman named Linda I met at a retreat. Linda and I had a fabulous discussion over lunch about the stirring of God she was beginning to sense. She is a teacher in her fifties. However, with her new roles as mother-in-law and grandma, she was learning much about relationships and mentoring. She sensed God leading her out of her teaching career and maybe into writing so she could share the truths and wisdom God had been teaching her. As she discussed her thoughts with me, I caught her tone of unbelief—*Surely not. How can this be? I'm not a writer. I'm a teacher.* The more she talked about the stirring in her, however, the more she was able to see God moving her and redirecting her toward a new, exciting phase of life.

Maybe part of the reason you have been reluctant to hear God or acknowledge his stirring in you is because you know you are not ready. The first half of this book laid the solid foundation to get you on your way to this dream. Now that you know who you are, who God is, and how to do relationships well, you can enter into the in-depth preparation necessary to pursue your dream.

Time with God

Preparation begins by taking time with God. Set aside a significant, regular time to spend with God. This needs to be a commitment. A hit-and-miss approach will not take you deeper with God, nor will you learn anything. It will barely maintain a limp status quo. If you don't have time for God, you don't have time to pursue the passion burning in your heart.

Another reason for a committed time with God is that the enemy has a neon target on your back. If you are going to stand strong and resist the enemy, you need to be faithful in the Word and meeting with God. You need to know him better and learn to hear his voice. In Isaiah 7:9 God gives us good reason to make time with him: "If you do not stand firm in your faith, you will not stand at all." We need this firm relationship with the Lord in order to be prepared not only for our calling but also to withstand the attacks of Satan. And they will come.

Ask God how he would have you study his Word. Many solid Bible studies can be done at home. Your church may offer a meaty study. Sometimes the temptation is to have a discussion or study around someone's ideas or philosophy rather than the Bible itself. So whatever you choose, make sure the study gets into the Word and discusses it.[42]

In your time with God, study the lives of other people God called and used to accomplish his awesome plan—Noah, Abraham, Joseph, Moses, Joshua, and David. Study their preparation—how God trained and shaped them to be the people he used for their amazing missions. Take note of the time they spent with God and how they interacted with him. Also note their ages when they were called, the length of their preparation, and then their ages when they fulfilled their missions. This research will help you better understand all that is involved in being called, prepared, and used by God.

Also study doctrine and theology. This means a study of the foundational truths of the Bible. It includes (but is not limited to) who God is, his character, the Trinity, the deity of Christ, the resurrection, salvation, the role of the Holy Spirit in our lives, and end times. Everything we think and do flows from these truths. They give us perspective on God and our relationship to him and his plan for us. You need a firm foundation in the Word to stand strong and be mightily used by God. I quickly learned that my enthusiasm wouldn't get me out my front door. Without a strong relationship with God and knowledge of his Word, I had nothing to build on—no strength, no boldness, no message, nothing to offer anyone.

Training

You may need more education to accomplish your dream. If your calling is to teach children in the inner city, you will need a teaching degree. If your calling is to be a nurse in a small country in Africa, you will need nurses' training. This takes time. God sets the timetable. He knew all the factors before you were born. Get in stride with the Lord.

Pruning

God also prepares our lives through pruning. Think of pruning a bush or tree; pruning starts with cutting out the dead branches. Do you have a bad habit eating up your time and money? Do you spend too much time on things that don't matter and don't produce? Pull your toes in, because I may step on them. The issue here is that you may have habits or activities that are keeping you from pursuing what God wants for you. Sometimes God requires us to say no to things even when they aren't wrong, immoral, or illegal. Sometimes he requires us to say no to certain amusements, while he allows other people to enjoy them. He sets us apart and waits to see our response.

Pruning is also cutting the excess out of our lives to make room for real growth that produces the fruit God designed us to produce. Some of us say yes to so many good things that we have no room for what God has called us to. Or we serve in our area of calling but not with excellence because we are doing too much elsewhere as well. Remember Ephesians 2:10? God planned our good works in advance for us to do. God has a specific plan for you. Doing other things is keeping you from that plan. If you say yes simply because no one else will volunteer, you are making yourself the savior. If you say yes to keep others happy with you, you are being a people pleaser, and that is idolatry. Both of these are sin.

When we say no to what is not our assignment from God, we are free to say yes to what *is* from God. Think of the opportunities that you knew were perfect for you—opportunities you were itching to do—but you had to say no because your life was too full of other things you couldn't say no to.

Not long ago I was talking with a woman who is a high-level leader for a large ministry. I admire her and her work; however, as we talked I learned how out of balance her life is. She talked on and on about stress due to taking on projects and responsibilities that she knew were not hers; she couldn't say no. As a result, both her family and her ministry suffer.

Princess, cooperate with God! Let him get rid of the dead branches and excess foliage that keep you from blooming and producing the fruit that is uniquely yours. The strong, confident princess accepts her calling and cooperates with God in pruning. Her life will look different from her peers' lives.

Are you bitter, sorry for yourself, or stomping your foot before God and demanding "fairness"? Or will you eagerly submit to God and his will for you and say, "God, I'm yours—my life is yours"? I am again reminded of Mary. After she heard everything the angel Gabriel told her about becoming the mother of the Messiah, she said, "I am the Lord's servant. . . . May it be to me as you have said" (Luke 1:38).

Mary gave up many good things to be the mother of Jesus. Rumors of an illegitimate birth haunted her life. She watched Jesus be misunderstood, rejected, and crucified. Her other children did not believe, at first, that Jesus was the Messiah. Will you accept your calling from God as Mary did and tell God, "I am your servant. May it be to me as you have said"?

Building a Testimony

Our preparation helps us build our testimony. Our *testimony* is how the world sees us live our faith. The world measures what we say about God by how we act and react, the decisions we make, the quality of our work, what we do when no one is looking, and if we are who we say we are. Without an authentic testimony, we cripple our calling.

I'm not saying we must be perfect at all times, but we must do our best to live what we say we believe. When we fail, we need to quickly admit our wrong to the one we offended, ask forgiveness, make right what we can, and then move on. We need to live humbly at the Lord's feet, not thinking more of ourselves than we should. "Do not think of yourself more highly than you ought, but rather think of yourself with sober judgment, in accordance with the measure of faith God has given you" (Romans 12:3). We need to be courteous to the clerk at the store, the secretary at our child's school, and the person who answers the phone at the insurance company—even when we've waited on hold for twenty minutes.

You are building your testimony every minute, every day, in every situation:

+ phone calls and e-mail (Ooh, be careful with e-mail—it can be passed around or sent to the wrong address.)
+ trips to town—your Jerusalem (see Acts 1:8)—to do errands
+ days on the job
+ volunteer hours at your child's school
+ time in the car (Please take the fish symbol off your car if you are an impatient, crazy driver!)

Every part of your life builds your testimony, and your testimony will be crucial in living the dream God has for you. You must be careful with it. A few years ago at a ministry event, I was introduced to a woman who said, "I saw you at Target a couple of weeks ago. I was behind you in line, and you had your girls with you." She smiled big.

My mind did a quick rewind. *When was I at Target? What kind of shopping day was I having with the girls? Were we happy or cranky at checkout?!*

She chatted on and kept smiling, so I assume the girls and I gave a favorable impression. But for a moment I did wonder. That incident made me realize that my world is not as big as I thought. People know me, and they know other people who know other people, and word gets around. I don't want to give the enemy a chance at taking me out of the game. I must resist the temptation to be anything but above reproach. Oh, don't even start to get the idea I walk around with a halo or that I think I am nearing perfect; I know the truth. That's why I must be alert, because I know the old, unprincessy me might try to seep out.

We will never be perfect until we meet the Lord, but we are called to live in a way that honors God. "As a prisoner for the Lord, then, I urge you to live a life worthy of the calling you have received" (Ephesians 4:1). We are called to do our best and leave the rest to God.

We build our testimony by building and protecting our character. Either we have solid character or we don't. On August 1, 2007, the I-35W bridge in Minneapolis, Minnesota, collapsed, killing 13 and injuring 145 people.[43] Experts identified weak gussets (the steel plates that hold the structure together) and corrosion as possible causes.[44] Both of these are unseen to the public. The thousands of people who crossed the bridge every day had no idea what was going on under the pavement. Yet because of the problems underneath, many lives were ended or devastated.

Our testimony needs to be made of sturdy material fastened to a deep foundation in Christ. Our character traits are the gusset plates. They hold together and support all we do. Our character is who we are. We build strong character by choosing and doing the right thing in situation after situation. Our character is built by thousands of little yeses to God:

+ "Yes, God, I will tell the whole truth and not keep back the part that makes me look bad."
+ "Yes, God, I will go back into the store and pay for the dozen eggs the computer didn't scan."
+ "Yes, God, I will clean my client's house impeccably, even though no one notices."
+ "Yes, God, I will guard my conversations with men so as not to appear to be a flirt or endanger my marriage."

Yes, God. Yes, God. One yes to God at a time—that is how we build character.

Even when we have sturdy character, we must guard against corrosion. Little things can slowly yet steadily tear down our character.

- One unforgiven offense takes a bitter root.
- One morsel of gossip tastes yummy, so we must have more.
- One viewing of illicit material on the Internet draws us back again and again.
- One flirty conversation with a man who is not ours turns emotionally intimate.
- One time of ignoring God's no to us makes it harder for us to be sensitive to him the next time.

Corrosion is subtle but dangerous! Often the biggest obstacle to fighting corrosion in our character is pride. We are too proud to admit we are tempted, too proud to ask a friend to pray for us and hold us accountable. We are too proud to ask for forgiveness. We are too proud to lay down *our* way and do life God's way.

Weak gusset plates and corrosion will bring down what appears to be a safe, massive bridge. Weak and corroding character will bring down even the most impressive-looking life.

Finding the Fabulous

We love God and want to fulfill the fabulous plan he has for us. Don't let it be lost because you are unwilling to grow in relationship with the King or get the junk out of your life. Stay strong, princess! Walk closely with your King, and you will see your character "take root below and bear fruit above" (2 Kings 19:30).

Looking Ahead

This week get serious about your relationship with God. Ask him to help you determine the best part of the day to have a committed time with him. Then commit to what he shows you. Get to know him in his Word and in prayer.

◆ ◆ ◆ ◆ ◆ ◆ ◆ ◆ ◆ ◆ ◆

DAY ONE: The King's Divine Plan for His Princess

God has called you to a specific plan—something that he put in your heart and something that he designed you to do. How have you processed that truth?

- ❏ I'm intrigued.
- ❏ I'm unbelieving.
- ❏ I'm fearful.
- ❏ I'm _____.

I love the force of this statement in Calvin Miller's book *The Power of Living for God's Pleasure*: "Only when we learn what we are to do and begin doing it—and keep on doing it—will we ever serve our world as God intended."[45] If you have been a person who serves wherever a need exists, whether or not you fit, how do this statement and this chapter change the way you will proceed in your service to God?

If you have not been active in service to God, how will you proceed now?

Before we move on to your exciting future, let's deal with the problem of serving God in a job that is not a good fit. I spent many years trying to serve God in children's ministry. Because I have the gift of teaching, it seemed the right fit. But oh no! My gifting is not teaching kids. I *am* passionate about children's ministry; it is crucial to do it well. The church needs to ground children in basic doctrine and teach them to apply it. But I am not naturally in tune with kids; I relate better to their mothers, grandmothers, and aunts. I finally caught on that children are not my area of service.

Describe a time when you were stuffed into a place of service that did not work for you.

Share what gifts were needed that you don't have or the passion needed that was not yours.

Maybe part of the problem was that you had responded to a friend's pleading for somebody to fill the position. That's what happened when I tried to teach children. The prophet Isaiah is a better example for us to follow. Read Isaiah 6:1-9. What was Isaiah's posture when he heard God speaking?

What was the attitude of Isaiah's heart when he realized he was in God's presence?

What was the result of the burning coal being touched to Isaiah's lips?

What happened immediately after that?

What did God say, and how did Isaiah respond?

Oswald Chambers has written about verse 8: "The call of God is not for the special few, it is for everyone. Whether or not I hear God's call depends upon the state of my ears; and what I hear depends upon my disposition."[46]

What is the "state of your ears"? Have you asked God to forgive your sins? Are you regularly in God's presence with eagerness to hear?

As we continue to get on board with God and his plan for us, let's dig into Ephesians 2:10 one more time. I love the way the *New American Standard Bible* words this verse: "We are His workmanship, created in Christ Jesus for good works, which God prepared beforehand so that we would walk in them." The phrase "walk in them" implies that pursuing and doing the vision God gives us will be a lifestyle for us. Doing what God made us to do is part of who we are. We make daily decisions in light of this passion. It took years for me to be able to say, "I am an author and speaker."

I had God's plan for me tucked into a tidy little pouch that I carried with me but rarely shared with others. I thought the dream was a fluke, so I kept it quiet. I did not consider God's character when I thought about his plan for me, so I doubted and was not confident.

Have you started to feel God's stirring and to hear his direction for you? What are you doing with it?

What is he showing you? (You don't have to share this with anyone now, but acknowledge here before God that you hear him speaking to you.)

Know that God's plan for you is real. It is not a fluke. Put all your excuses to the side for a moment. If God has put a stirring in you—given you a glimpse of his plan for you—what are you thinking or feeling?

How can you see yourself doing what God has shown you? Can you sense his delight in your doing what he made you to do?

In the movie *Chariots of Fire*, the Olympic British runner Eric Liddell knew his purpose. He said, "I believe God made me for a purpose, but he also made me fast. And when I run I feel His pleasure."[47] In that moment of knowing what God called you to, did you feel his pleasure? If God has nudged you toward your dream, please know it pleases, even delights him when you do the thing he created you to do. If he has not yet stirred you, stay at his feet. Pray. Seek God. Know him better. We want to keep God as our focus rather than focusing on our dream, our job, our families, or our church. God only.

✦ ✦ ✦ ✦ ✦ ✦ ✦ ✦ ✦ ✦ ✦

DAY TWO: The Princess Discovers Her Father's Plan for Her

Today we will talk about the pieces of your dream. As I shared yesterday, I mistakenly served in children's ministry for years before I realized that is not my passion. Yes, I am passionate about children, but I am convinced that the best way for me to help children is to encourage and teach mothers. I am passionate that women know God's truth, including what he says about their role as moms. I have a dear friend who is passionate about getting the Bible into every language so all people can read God's Word. She and her family live in Africa, working on materials to teach reading to the tribes of Senegal. The Bible is incorporated into those materials.

Who or what are you passionate about? If you could make a difference for anyone or any cause, what would it be?

God's calling does not mean volunteer work only. God may be directing you to a career in your calling. Pauline is an inspiring woman in my church. She is a teacher in an inner-city school. She shows Jesus to her students every day.

The next piece to putting your dream together is discovering your spiritual gifts. Define *spiritual gift* in your own words.

Discovering our spiritual gifts is essential to knowing what the King made us to do. Calvin Miller says it perfectly: "To fail to know what our gifts are will keep us wandering around for a lifetime, not knowing what God has given us to do to please him."[48] Look back at the list of some of the spiritual gifts. For a more thorough listing of spiritual gifts, read 1 Corinthians 12:7-10, 28; Ephesians 4:11; and Romans 12:6-8. Which one(s) have you experienced God working through you?

If you know your spiritual gift(s), list them here.

Calvin Miller provides one more encouragement to discover and use our gifts: "Until we are doing what God has gifted us to do, we will not be doing what God has called us to do."[49] Right about now I imagine some strong-willed princesses are digging in their heels and saying, "I'm not doing this spiritual-gift stuff, and she can't make me." If this is you, tell God here why you don't want to seek out the gifts he gave you to use for his unique plan for you.

If you don't know your gifts but have an inkling, list what you think they might be.

If you don't have a clue but are ready to discover them, make that commitment here.

How will you proceed in discovering your spiritual gifts?

I also urge you to do a study on spiritual gifts or at least take a spiritual gifts test.[50] Let's end today by putting together what you have discovered about yourself. Has

God been stirring you regarding a certain area of service or certain people? Has he brought back to your mind a dream he gave you years ago? List those here.

Put this all together. With your passion, your gifting, and talents, how do you see God moving you toward your dream?

Go to the Royal Truths and list what you learned about yourself today.

✦ ✦ ✦ ✦ ✦ ✦ ✦ ✦ ✦ ✦ ✦

DAY THREE: The Princess Begins Preparing for Her Mission

We can learn much from Elijah the prophet in the Old Testament. God was about to do something supernatural through Elijah. "The power of the LORD came upon Elijah" (1 Kings 18:46). Elijah knew God was up to something big. Verse 46 also tells us what Elijah did in response—he "tuck[ed] his cloak into his belt." Elijah prepared himself for what God was going to do through him. Then he was ready, and "he ran ahead of Ahab all the way to Jezreel." Before you yawn here, look back at verses 44, 45. Ahab was traveling fast in a chariot, trying to get off the mountain before a big rain came. Elijah, empowered by God, passed Ahab and his horse-drawn chariot! Elijah was ready for this amazing feat because he prepared himself when God began to stir him.

On Day One I asked you to consult with God regarding a time committed to meeting with him. How is that coming?

If you don't think you have time to meet with God, your priorities are out of whack. Even Jesus took time to meet with his Father while he was living his earthly life. "Jesus often withdrew to the wilderness for prayer" (Luke 5:16, *NLT*). Jesus went to his Father before his most difficult mission—his crucifixion: "Jesus came with them to a place called Gethsemane, and said to His disciples, 'Sit here while I go over there and pray'" (Matthew 26:36, *NASB*).

What is the biggest obstacle keeping you from time with God for prayer and Bible study?

What changes will you make so that time with God will be a regular part of your day? (If nothing is coming to mind, will you talk to God about his solution?)

Now it's time to start getting even more personal. Maybe the reason you don't have time for God is that your life needs some pruning. Maybe you have too much junk taking up valuable time. What do you waste too much time on? Write it down. (That first thing that came to your mind but you drew it back—that's it.)

Hold it out to God and see if this is something God wants you to limit or to remove permanently. How might that play out?

Paul teaches us this principle: "'Everything is permissible for me'—but not everything is beneficial. 'Everything is permissible for me'—but I will not be mastered by anything" (1 Corinthians 6:12). What is permissible *and* beneficial in your life?

What is permissible but *not* beneficial in your life?

What is permissible but mastering you?

I know this hurts and doesn't seem fair. But God doesn't take away anything that is good for us. Remember his agape love for us. "Those who seek the Lord lack no good thing" (Psalm 34:10). Talk to God about what you are cutting out of your life, trusting him to use this action for good in his plan for you. Note your thoughts here if you like.

One More Thing

Princess Unaware, I'm so proud of you! This is hard work. You are doing it well. Many believers don't get as far as you are today. I'm excited about where God is taking you.

✦ ✦ ✦ ✦ ✦ ✦ ✦ ✦ ✦ ✦ ✦

DAY FOUR: The Princess Learns the World Is Watching

The world watches Christians. We need to be alert, not to guard against embarrassment but to honor our Lord in our lives. We want to be what we say we are so the world will listen when we speak about God. I believe that hypocrisy in Christians is a major reason the world disregards Christianity.

Describe a time when you did or said something in public and hoped no one was watching.

The I-35W bridge collapse in 2007 was likely caused by weak gusset plates and corrosion. If gusset plates represent character issues in our lives, name a few gusset plates that you believe make a strong foundation.

Which of those characteristics are you strong in?

Which of those characteristics do you need to decide to improve in?

Corrosion is gradual deterioration. Paul challenged us to guard against corrosion in our lives: "Let us not be like others, who are asleep, but let us be alert and self-controlled. For those who sleep, sleep at night, and those who get drunk, get drunk at night. But since we belong to the day, let us be self-controlled, putting on faith and love as a breastplate, and the hope of salvation as a helmet" (1 Thessalonians 5:6-8).

Where do you lack self-control?

How does this allow corrosion in your character and your testimony? Share that with God here.

Read 1 Peter 5:8, 9. We cannot ignore the truth that the enemy is after us. How does self-control paired with alertness enable us to protect our testimonies?

Explain how being self-controlled and alert will help you "stand firm in the faith" in your area of weakness.

Give this area of weakness to God. Let him take it. Write your plan and, if you can, a verse to use the next time the situation or temptation comes.

Now write today's date. Let this be a spiritual marker in your relationship with God.

I could fill the rest of this book with stories of famous people who looked great and spiritual on the outside, but no one knew how weak their "gusset plates" were or how they were allowing "corrosion" in their lives. The weak and corroded parts of their lives that they thought would stay private gained national headlines, and their lives and big dream from God crashed. I don't want that to be me. I don't want that to be you. Maybe you need to talk to someone about your issue. If you are in a group, ask your leader for help or find a professional Christian counselor. It will be a huge investment in the rest of your life.

Let this verse be your final challenge this week: "Whatever happens, conduct yourselves in a manner worthy of the gospel of Christ" (Philippians 1:27).

Looking Back

How did the week go? Are you getting an idea of your talents, spiritual gifts, and the calling God has for you?

What challenged you most this week?

What encouraged or excited you most?

How is your relationship with God changing or growing?

Princess Unaware, you are becoming more of what your Father designed you to be—a strong, confident princess. I'm proud of you!

chapter seven
What Royal Success Looks Like

The Princess Defines
Her Priorities

Princess Jessica awoke, stretched, and looked out her window. She found the sun high in the sky and her sisters in the courtyard, sparring with swords. She furrowed her brow. Weren't princesses supposed to learn the fine art of serving tea and making light conversation?

From the doorway, a deep voice startled her from her thoughts. "Good morning, Jessica."

"Father!" She ran to him, somewhat undecided whether to embrace him or bow. "Father, what are my sisters doing down there with the knights? It seems . . . quite unladylike."

"You will be joining them shortly."

"But I don't have anything to wear for such activity."

"The closet is filled with beautiful dresses just for you. However, for the morning session you will find a tunic and leggings." The King left Jessica to dress.

Tunic and leggings? How manly! she thought as she put them on.

Jessica timidly opened her door and made sure no one was coming before she sneaked to the staircase that led down to the inner courtyard where her sisters were. Jessica felt embarrassed wearing only wool leggings on her legs.

"Jessica! Jessica! Jessica!" The girls smothered their newfound sister with hugs.

"Is this your normal morning routine?" she asked.

"Oh . . . sometimes. But sometimes we take long rides through the mountains. Sometimes we practice archery."

"I don't understand. All of this is terribly unprincesslike."

"On the contrary, dear Jessica," said one of the sisters and, seeing Father approaching, added, "Isn't that right, Father?"

"Yes," answered Father, "your training as princess goes much deeper than pretty dresses and courtly rituals."

"It does?" Jessica asked.

"You will be trained extensively in weaponry—both mine and the enemy's. I will teach you how to follow my lead. Your parents taught you integrity and strength of character. It will be crucial in all your training."

"Training . . ." she said.

"Finally, dear daughter, you will learn what is appropriate dress for each situation you face, for every encounter."

Jessica looked unsure. "Encounter . . ." she repeated.

"But don't worry," the King added with a smile. "You will also wear all the beautiful dresses in your closet."

Like Princess Jessica, we are easily confused about what our success as princesses of the King should look like. Our culture looks at money, appearance, possessions, family, and career to measure success.

The Christian community gets drawn into those measurements plus many other criteria that we shouldn't even be measuring. How many people attended a church service, concert, or special event? How many accepted Christ? How many did the Christian homeless shelter serve? How many babies were saved by the crisis pregnancy center? We measure the success of those who teach us by reciting their long list of degrees and accomplishments. How many books did they write? How many CDs were sold?

How would Jesus have responded to such questions about his success?

- ✦ "Jesus, wow, you made lots of bread and fish today. As a result, how many souls responded to that miracle?"
- ✦ "Jesus, how you healed that leper was amazing! The latest polls show that 84 percent of the people believe it was a real miracle and, as a result, placed their faith in you. How do you feel about that number?"
- ✦ "Jesus, can you hear me from up on that cross? How does this crucifixion coincide with your plan to be King of the Jews?"

No, Jesus wasn't into numbers, polls, or obvious results. He was all about his mission. I'll let Jesus define his success:

- "My food . . . is to do the will of him who sent me and to finish his work" (John 4:34).
- "By myself I can do nothing; I judge only as I hear, and my judgment is just, for I seek not to please myself but him who sent me" (John 5:30).
- "The very work that the Father has given me to finish, and which I am doing, testifies that the Father has sent me" (John 5:36).
- "I have come down from heaven not to do my will but to do the will of him who sent me" (John 6:38).
- "Later, knowing that all was now completed, and so that the Scripture would be fulfilled, Jesus said, 'I am thirsty.' . . . When he had received the drink, Jesus said, 'It is finished.' With that, he bowed his head and gave up his spirit" (John 19:28, 30).

That's not the way the world defines success. Yes, we know this isn't the end of the story, but to the world it was the end—and not a successful one.

Jesus' life was successful, however, because he completely fulfilled the mission God put him on earth to do (John 19:28). We will gauge the success of our lives the same way. This is why it is crucial for each of us to know God, know who we are in Christ, and know the specific dream he has for each of us. Without all of this, we will be missing the point of why we are here, and our lives will not fulfill their purpose.

Define It!

Jesus understood his ministry. In John 2:1-11 Jesus and his family were guests at a wedding. The wine ran out before the celebration was finished. Mary, Jesus' mother, told him about the problem. Jesus instructed the servants to fill huge jars with water, jars normally used for ceremonial washing. He told them to take a cup of it to the master of the banquet. It was wine, and not just wine, but excellent wine. Verse 11 tells us Jesus' purposes in the miracle—to "[reveal] his glory" and so "his disciples [would] put their faith in him."

Not only did Jesus understand his ministry, he knew what was *not* his ministry.

Jesus did not heal every sick person while he was on the earth. He did not right all wrongs. He did not deliver the Jews from Roman rule. Jesus knew that for his life to be successful, he would need to do what his Father gave him to do, nothing more and nothing less.

Jesus also defined success by relationships. Jesus taught crowds of people; however, a close examination of the Gospels reveals that the people who were most affected by Jesus experienced him one-on-one or in small groups. These people more often repented and lived changed lives. (I'm not discrediting the value of teaching a large crowd. In the book of Acts, we see thousands being added to the family of God, sometimes daily, after the apostles preached. But I don't want us to miss the power of Jesus in relationships. That is another way Jesus measured success.)

Jesus maintained focus on his mission because he had his priorities in order. In the Gospels we see Jesus healing and teaching people, setting aside time for teaching and doing life with his disciples, relaxing with friends, and even verbally dueling with the Pharisees. In John 7:1-9 we see Jesus stating his priorities to his unbelieving brothers. They challenged him to go to the Feast of Tabernacles to show off his miracles. They didn't believe he was the Messiah. Their words dripped with jealousy and sarcasm: "No one who wants to become a public figure acts in secret. Since you are doing these things, show yourself to the world" (v. 4). Jesus responded graciously, "The right time for me has not yet come" (v. 6). Jesus knew his priorities for his ministry. He defended them and lived them.

If we are going to fulfill the plan God has for us, we'll need to determine our priorities. We cannot do everything that comes our way. Defining our priorities will help us know what is God's plan for us and what is not.

Let's start with basic life priorities that we need no matter what our calling is. It took me several years to develop mine, but I am confident you can do this much faster. In my first book, *Queen Mom*, I listed my own priorities. They haven't changed because they are from God and are good for my growing (and aging!) life. Here they are:

+ keeping my relationship with God daily, fresh, and honest

- giving my husband and girls quality time and as much quantity as I can when they are home (this includes staying on top of my home chores)
- serve God through my God-given passion
- spend time with my friends and extended family

My life constantly changes. The girls are growing up and becoming independent, and circumstances change. But my priorities don't change. For example, our oldest daughter Katie has been living on her own for three years. When she comes home for a visit, she is still my priority. I make sure I am there and have snacks when she comes in the door. (I wonder if she ever eats or only waits for Mom's goodies!) Even though she is not under our roof, she is still my daughter, and she is still my priority.

What will your list of priorities look like? We will work on this in the study section of this chapter, but start thinking now about who and what will go on your list. You may need to add caring for an aging parent or a disabled family member. You may need to add job responsibilities. Prayerfully consider your list. Our world is full of choices, and we need priorities to help us know which ones are for us.

Jesus knew to say no when an opportunity wasn't his, and he didn't have a problem saying no. Can you get your tongue to touch the roof of your mouth right behind your front teeth and make your lips form an O shape? I'll give you a minute to practice. Go ahead. Now say, "NO-O-O." There, you got it! Practice it throughout the day. Then the next time someone asks you to do something, run it through your priorities; and if it doesn't make the cut, say no.

When you say no, you are setting boundaries around God's unique plan for you. You are telling the world, "My life is special and planned by God, and I'm intent on living it successfully." Jesus set boundaries with his brothers. They said, "Go to the feast." Jesus said, "Not now." End of discussion. Setting priorities and boundaries gives you freedom to do what God intended for you. You won't be at anyone's beck and call except God's.

The strong, confident princess knows her success depends on setting and living her priorities and boundaries.

Live It!

You are doing great, Princess Unaware. You either know your mission from God, or you are in a posture to hear him when his time is right. You have defined success and set your priorities. But this is where I see many women losing it. They want what God has for them, but they don't want to do the heavy lifting necessary to successfully live God's plan for them. Let's look at some of what that hard work requires.

Excellence

First, our lives must shine with excellence. Excellence is knowing what needs to be done and doing it as well and as thoroughly as we can. When we have done this, we are satisfied and content in our work.

Excellence is not overcompensating. When Jesus healed people, he didn't follow them home to make sure they lived righteous lives. He didn't go into their homes, clean for them, and make sure they were eating healthy to continue to take care of the body he'd miraculously healed. Jesus did what he was called to do for them, and then he moved on.

Excellence also is not perfectionism. Perfectionism is never satisfied with its efforts. It never feels like it has done its best; therefore, it is never confident. Excellence seeks to honor God. Perfectionism seeks to honor self.

Jesus did everything with excellence. Remember when Jesus turned the water to wine at the wedding? The master of the banquet complimented the groom on the wine: "Everyone brings out the choice wine first and then the cheaper wine after the guests have had too much to drink; but you have saved the best till now" (John 2:10). The wine Jesus made was the best. Jesus fed crowds of thousands with just a little food. Each time the disciples picked up many basketfuls of leftovers (Mark 6:30-44; 8:1-9). When Jesus healed someone, he not only healed an impossible physical condition; he also forgave sins (Matthew 9:1-7). Jesus did God's mission for him with excellence.

Excellence is rare in today's society. Mediocrity is being accepted as the new normal, so when I experience someone doing her job with excellence, I take notice.

A couple of years ago, I was shopping for the perfect pair of dress boots. I don't wear black, and I was having a terrible time finding my perfect pair of boots in brown. I visited the department store in my city, known for its large selection of shoes. I found a pair of boots I loved, but the store only carried them in black. The saleswoman offered to search the store's database to see if another store in the chain might have them. After a few minutes, she located the boots in brown in my size at a store out of state. She immediately called the store and ordered them for me. I got the sale price and no delivery charge. Imagine my over-the-top excitement! I expressed my appreciation. Then I went up to the management offices and asked to talk to the manager. I told him what a great employee he had working in his store. His response was apathetic. He couldn't even look me in the eyes for the duration of our brief conversation. How sad. This fabulous woman was doing an excellent job serving her customers. Too bad she had a mediocre manager who did not care.

Whether we are selling shoes, changing a diaper, doing heart surgery, or translating the Bible for the people of a tiny African village, we are doing it all for God, and we must do it with excellence. "Whatever you do, work at it with all your heart, as working for the Lord, not for men" (Colossians 3:23).

Details

Doing our best also means tending to the details. Little things matter. Reply to correspondence promptly; no one likes waiting on an answer. If you don't know the answer, let the other person know you are working on it and will get back to her soon. Be punctual. Habitual lateness says two things: "I am not self-disciplined" and "I am more important than you." Punctuality catches attention. We want the ever-watching world to see us honoring our Lord. Then they will continue to watch us live out our testimonies—and be more willing to listen to our words.

Show equal respect to each person you come in contact with. That's what Jesus did. He treated social outcasts, Roman soldiers, and women with the same respect that Jewish leaders expected for themselves.

Tending to the details also means no shortcuts. Do a thorough job. Neatness counts. My friend's husband is a doctor in a large group practice. She shared with me her husband's dismay over the condition of young doctors' job applications and résumés. These young men and women had devoted years of intensive study and work to become doctors. Yet the first impression given to their prospective employer was messy, poorly done, and unprofessional.

Last night Kelsey came home from a babysitting job excited about the generous check she received. "Mom, I made forty dollars, and I was there less than four hours!" Later in the conversation she told me how she'd cleaned up the dinner mess, picked up after the kids, and tidied the house. I told her, "I'm sure that's why the parents were so generous." Kelsey not only watched the children, she tended to the details. Her excellence was noticed and rewarded.

The importance of tending to details dovetails into our character development also. Two areas of our lives are invisibly linked; true character is linked to the mouth. Jesus told those gnarly Pharisees, "You brood of vipers, how can you who are evil say anything good? For out of the overflow of the heart the mouth speaks" (Matthew 12:34). Ouch! Are we ready for that truth? Think about the times a celebrity or politician has said something offensive or crude, thinking his microphone was off. The overflow of his heart revealed his true self. This is one reason why we need to clean up our character and also ask God to "set a guard over [our] mouth[s], O LORD; keep watch over the door[s] of [our] lips" (Psalm 141:3).

God's plan is for us to be perfect as he is: "Be perfect, therefore, as your heavenly Father is perfect" (Matthew 5:48). In this verse *perfect* means "complete (in various applications of labor, growth, mental and moral character)."[51] So God will be alerting us to the various areas we need to clean up.

At first God may pick on obvious areas, but as you progress it may seem that he is picking on every little deficit in character. The sins you used to privately enjoy will now be spoiled by constant prickling from the Holy Spirit. At times I have opened my mouth to say something I shouldn't, and I have heard "uh-uh" from the Holy Spirit. But I dismissed him and kept on talking, and all the while I heard the Holy Spirit saying, "Stop. Don't say that. Stop." And on and on I kept talking. Ugh, I can be so stubborn. But after a number of near-fatal crashes caused by my mouth, I committed myself to not sharing people's personal information with others. Confidentiality is crucial to solid character. People will decide by what comes out of your mouth whether they can trust you. If you are sharing gossip or someone's personal information, they will know they can't share confidential information with you. Anything you do for God requires that you can be trusted with private information.

James, Jesus' half brother, wrote about the power of our words:

> A bit in the mouth of a horse controls the whole horse. A small rudder on a huge ship in the hands of a skilled captain sets a course in the face of the strongest winds. A word out of your mouth may seem of no account, but it can accomplish nearly anything—or destroy it! It only takes a spark, remember, to set off a forest fire. A careless or wrongly placed word out of your mouth can do that. By our speech we can ruin the world, turn harmony to chaos, throw mud on a reputation, send the whole world up in smoke and go up in smoke with it, smoke right from the pit of hell (James 3:3-6, *The Message*).

Our character needs integrity. Our words will reveal our integrity. All of our hard work and good efforts will be wasted if we cannot keep our mouths under control. Resist the temptation to offer the inside information you have. At times I have almost had to clamp my jaws shut to keep safe the sensitive information I was privy to. Sometimes the information would have defended the person being judged, but I sat without saying a word. I fought my deep desire for truth to be told, because anything I said would have revealed that I knew something; but the information had been given to me in confidence and was not mine to share. (However, in a situation involving someone's safety, a legal matter, or circumstances requiring church discipline, we are biblically safe go to the proper authority.)

Appearance

You've worked hard to become the princess God designed you to be—allowing God to direct you, prune you, and sharpen your character. You're working hard to build and protect your testimony so the watching world will catch a glimpse of Jesus through you and be drawn closer to God. Are you also presenting an appearance that reflects your excellence in character? Oswald Chambers makes a pithy comment about appearance: "They are careless about what they wear, and they look as they have no business to look."[52] What does your appearance say about you? How does it reflect Jesus?

I faithfully watch *What Not to Wear* on TLC. The hosts of the program help women (nominated by friends and family) shop and find their look; then each one gets a new hairstyle and makeup too. Most often the women having the makeovers are resistant at first. Their attitudes change on the day Stacy and Clinton help them shop and put together their new outfits. By the time their hair and makeup are done, they see the best in themselves, and even their outlook on life changes. As Christians we have much more to represent to the world than just ourselves. We are representing our Savior, his gospel, and eternal life.

First, in your quest toward a quality appearance, look relevant.[53] What looked fabulous on you ten years ago now dates you. Even if the suit you wore in the 1980s is still in perfect condition, when you wear it now, the world will see you as out of touch with current culture and will stop listening.

Next, dress appropriately for your age. This past year I turned forty-nine. I can no longer do the trendy, casual look that might leave strangers wondering if I'm my daughters' sister or young aunt. (It did happen one time, and my daughter was not happy! I think the guy needed glasses.) My age and body demanded a transition in my look so as not to reveal my back fat (ugh!) or give the impression that I think I am twenty-something or thirty-something. And no way do I want to look older than I am. It is a fine line.

The benefit of doing the necessary work to look my best is that it saves me time and money. My clothes coordinate, so I have more outfits with less expense and I don't spend much time shopping. I get what I need; then I am free to live my fabulous princess life without fretting about how I look.

Pursue It

Now it's time to think about pursuing your calling. I have already said that I had thought God would bring opportunities to me as I sat on my dream, waiting for it to hatch. Not so. I had to follow God's leading. Abraham did the same thing. "The LORD had said to Abram, 'Leave your country, your people and your father's household and go to the land I will show you.' . . . So Abram left, as the LORD had told him" (Genesis 12:1, 4).

Follow God's Leading ☂

My young neighbor Jennifer received a similar word from God. She was living an exciting life of ministry through her photography, but God had another direction for her. For a couple of years, he had been impressing on her the need to pursue publishing a book of her incredible photographs of the Holy Land. She did not know where to begin. She was content and happy in her current ministry, but God would not let up on her. One day Jennifer called and asked, "Can I come over and talk about getting a book published?" Oh, how exciting!

Two hours evaporated as I shared all I knew for her to do in order to follow God's leading. I also challenged her to acknowledge that God was truly directing her and to get on board with this mission from God. She followed my advice. It has been about five months since our first conversation. Jennifer has signed with one of the most respected agents in Christian publishing, and he is working on several viable opportunities for her book.

Jennifer listened to God's call; then she followed it the best way she knew—by talking with someone who could help her take the next step. She followed the plan God gave her through the red-headed lump of clay who lives next door. God was waiting for Jennifer to get on board so he could start doing his amazing thing!

Pursue Opportunities from God ☂

The next way we pursue God's vision for us is by pursuing the opportunities he brings to us that are in line with his vision. Peter was a fisherman when Jesus called him to the life he was made to live (Mark 1:16-18). For three years Peter followed Jesus. He learned from him; he watched Jesus do life, relate to people, relate to his Father, mourn, eat, and celebrate. After all that, he failed Jesus on two different occasions—once in the Garden of Gethsemane and then in the courtyard of the high priest (Mark 14). But Jesus still had plans for Peter.

After the resurrection, Jesus met up with Peter and some of the other disciples while they were fishing and wondering what would happen next. They sat around a fire, eating the breakfast Jesus had prepared. Then Jesus turned the conversation to Peter: "'Do you truly love me more than these?' 'Yes, Lord,' he said, 'you know that I love you.' Jesus said, 'Feed my lambs'" (John 21:15). Two more times Jesus asked Peter that question, and each time Peter said yes. Each time Jesus responded with Peter's new ministry: "Feed my lambs. . . . Take care of my sheep. . . . Feed my sheep." Jesus punctuated this with, "Follow me!" (vv. 15-19). Peter had his orders from Jesus. What would he do with them? The book of Acts shows us that Peter became a prominent leader in the church. He preached and healed. He also was arrested and put in prison. He didn't do everything perfectly, but he persevered in the opportunities God brought to him.

No opportunity is too small if it comes from God. In my journey God has brought me opportunities that seemed small but led to other opportunities. In a couple of months, I will be speaking at a women's event with the chance to touch the lives of hundreds of women. I can trace this opportunity back to a shopping day with my sister. While waiting for my sister to try on outfit after outfit, the saleswoman and I started a conversation. Then came the common question, "So . . . what do you do?" I answered that I was a mom, author, and speaker. Unexpectedly, the woman asked me to come to speak to her professional group. Through this opportunity God brought other opportunities that led to this event.

I have a couple of cautions concerning opportunities. First, don't bite at everything. Trust God's leading or his cautioning not to proceed. A good question to ask is, Does this opportunity fall in line with my gifting and passion? Second, review your predetermined priorities as you consider the opportunity. God will not have us sacrifice our families in order to say yes to everything that comes our way.

Pay Attention to Timing

One final consideration in pursuing our calling is timing. The timing is from God. Oswald Chambers advises us, "Let God fling you out, and do not go until He does. If you select your own spot, you will prove an empty pod. If God sows you, you will bring forth fruit."[54] As you develop your relationship with God, you will learn to hear his voice and get in his stride. Stay there. Resist the temptation to run ahead. Well-meaning loved ones may encourage you to take charge of your dream. But this isn't a new business; this is God's vision for you. Stay at his feet. Move when he says move, and wait when he says wait. I jokingly tell people God has me on a short leash at his feet, because he knows if he gave me too much rope I would run too far ahead of him, wrap myself around a mailbox post, and be stuck. (This illustration is compliments of my dog.)

Even Jesus knew to wait on God's timing for his ministry. Remember Jesus' conversation with his brothers? They were taunting him to run ahead of God. Let's reread part of it from *The Message*: "His brothers said, 'Why don't you leave here and go up to the Feast so your disciples can get a good look at the works you do? No one who intends to be publicly known does everything behind the scenes. If you're serious about what you are doing, come out in the open and show the world.' His brothers were pushing him like this because they didn't believe in him either" (John 7:3-5). But Jesus was in tune with his Father. He knew it wasn't time. Stay in God's stride.

I must add one more thing. Be careful of the comparison trap. Again Oswald Chambers has wisdom for us: "You have to walk in the light of the vision that has been given to you and not compare yourself with others or judge them, that is between them and God."[55] Your calling is yours. My calling is mine. Jennifer's is hers. We can't change it. We are doubting God's sovereignty when we want what our sister has. The strong, confident princess knows what her success looks like. She boldly lives the unique life her Father has given her.

Finding the Fabulous

 ## Looking Ahead

This week think about how you can paraphrase John 6:38 to apply to defining success for you God's way. Here is John 6:38 and my own paraphrase: "I have come down from heaven (for me it is from Germantown Hills, Illinois) not to do my will (Brenda G's big plan that would crash and burn immediately after takeoff) but to do the will of him who sent me (day by day doing the next thing God puts in front of me)."

✦ ✦ ✦ ✦ ✦ ✦ ✦ ✦ ✦ ✦ ✦

DAY ONE: Success Redefined

Before you'd read this chapter, how did you define success? Be honest.

Jesus challenged the way the world and the religious establishment did business. He didn't fall into their way of thinking or living. That includes the way he defined success. Think about the vision God has given you. What or where is he calling you to?

Remember that this vision is not only to benefit others through you but also to help you become "perfect [or complete], therefore, as your heavenly Father is perfect" (Matthew 5:48).

Write a few sentences of prayer, interacting with the truth in the following verses about doing God's will God's way with regard to your calling and life.

John 4:34

John 5:30

John 5:36

John 6:38

How did this exercise help you redefine success Jesus' way?

Reread John 19:28, 30. If you were an onlooker at the crucifixion, what would have been your estimation of the life of the one who called himself the Messiah?

God's plans do not have to make sense to the onlookers in the world. Let's take a look at the calling of a great Old Testament prophet, Ezekiel. Read Ezekiel 2:1–3:9. Put a little checkmark in your Bible beside each time God told Ezekiel how rebellious and hard Israel was (I counted eleven).

In 3:3 how does Ezekiel describe the words God gave him to speak to Israel?

Even though God thoroughly explained the difficulties Ezekiel would face, the mission God gave him was sweet when he consumed it. Write your thoughts on these two truths of fulfilling God's plan for you—the difficulty of not always seeing results and the sweetness of living God's will for you.

Jesus also defined success by relationships. He made the most impact in people's lives when he was one-on-one with them or in small groups. Read Matthew 13:36-43. What was the setting and situation?

Read Matthew 9:18-26. List the who, what, where, and when of Jesus' miracle in these verses.

Jesus taught the disciples the meaning of his parables after they drew away from the crowds. He went to the home of a synagogue ruler to bring the ruler's dead daughter back to life.

Phil Vischer, the creator of VeggieTales, tells in *Me, Myself, & Bob* about the conception, rise, and subsequent loss of his company, Big Idea. Through his experience, Vischer learned what Jesus taught about relationships and success: "Real impact today comes from building great relationships, not huge organizations."[56] Relationships are key to defining success Christ's way. The strong, confident princess defines success her Father's way.

✦ ✦ ✦ ✦ ✦ ✦ ✦ ✦ ✦ ✦ ✦

DAY TWO: Priorities Defined

I believe women struggle with defining and living their priorities more than men do. Women don't like to say no, and we understand that if we set priorities, something or someone will be on the bottom or will not make the list. If we don't have priorities, we won't have to say no. But the reality is, we can't do or be everything we are asked to do and be. We must say no even to some good things so the best will thrive.

Jesus had priorities. He had no trouble telling others what those priorities were—and living them. Quickly list who or what is important to you.

Now prioritize that list—who or what gets your best or overrules another?

Think over the past six months. What does the reality of your daily life reveal to be your priorities? List them in order.

What are the similarities and differences in the two lists?

In prayer show these lists to God. Ask God what he wants on your list and where he wants it. Don't argue with him. Just write it down when you sense his leading. This exercise is the beginning of a process. You don't have to know right now all the details of how God will work it out.

Remember, Jesus valued his relationship with his Father and his disciples, friends, and family. He lived to do the mission God gave him.

 ## One More Thing

Jesus lived for approximately thirty-three years. His ministry was about three years long. For thirty years he was living what we would consider a normal life. But he was still living his Father's will—for example, developing relationships, working hard, and taking care of Mary after Joseph died.

Now that your priorities are in order, you will need to defend them and live them. This means you will have to set boundaries. Boundaries are not to separate you from the world; they are to keep you on track with the life God planned for you. Often Jesus had to defend his boundaries to stay on track with God. If he didn't, the people's desires would have been running his life. Read John 6:30-42. In verses 30, 31, what were people asking Jesus to do?

How did Jesus respond (v. 32)? Did they get it (v. 34)?

Read through verse 52. How well was Jesus' truth received?

The crowds wanted a show from Jesus—"If you are the Christ, if you really care about us, show us." Describe a time that your boundaries were challenged in that way—"If you really care about me, you will . . ." or "If you are a good Christian, you will . . ."

How did you respond? (Hey, we have all been there and we have all fallen for it, so don't be ashamed if you gave in.)

In *Queen Mom* I wrote about the need to defend the priorities and boundaries we have for our families. This means we will have to say no. Do you have trouble saying no? Explain your answer.

Read John 11:1-37. When was word sent to Jesus to come to the home of Lazarus?

What did Jesus do in response to the request (vv. 4-6)?

What expectations of Jesus did Martha, Mary, and the Jews have (vv. 21, 32, 37)?

Now read through verse 45. What was Jesus' purpose in delaying his arrival, which resulted in the death of Lazarus (vv. 11, 14, 15, 23, 43, 44)?

What was the result of Jesus' raising Lazarus from the dead (v. 45)?

What would have happened if Jesus had gone immediately to Lazarus's home and healed him?

God's plan for Jesus would not have been fulfilled had Jesus followed the people's wishes. Jesus knew that, and he said, "No, it is for God's glory so that God's Son may be glorified through it" (v. 4). Process this biblical truth—God has a call on your life. Why is it important to know what's from God and to be able to say no to everything else?

If you're doing this study with a group, pair off and briefly role-play saying no to each other. One person plays a sweet yet persistent person in need of a volunteer or help; the other person plays herself, knowing that this opportunity is not from God for her.

✦ ✦ ✦ ✦ ✦ ✦ ✦ ✦ ✦ ✦ ✦

DAY THREE: Live It!

Are you starting to get a clear vision of the person God created you to be and what he has for you? I am excited for you. Now that you are taking "hold of that for which Christ Jesus took hold of [us]" (Philippians 3:12), you need to live it well. This will require some heavy lifting on your part.

Define *excellence* in your own words.

Finish this sentence: Excellence is not

Describe a time when Jesus did something in your life with excellence—beyond what you expected and with better results than you could have imagined.

How does Colossians 3:23 define excellence?

Excellence has many pieces that seem insignificant individually. Briefly describe the importance of excellence in the following "details." How do you rate in each area?

replying promptly to correspondence

being punctual

treating everyone with equal respect

not taking shortcuts

neatness

Our character is most truthfully revealed in the way we speak. "For out of the overflow of the heart the mouth speaks," Jesus tells us (Matthew 12:34). Explain the necessity of allowing God to clean up our character and make us perfect "as [our] heavenly Father is perfect" (Matthew 5:48).

Paul instructs us, "Do not let any unwholesome talk come out of your mouths, but only what is helpful for building others up according to their needs, that it may benefit those who listen" (Ephesians 4:29). In what way do you find unwholesome talk coming out of your mouth—curse words, gossip, negative or trash talk, lying, coarse joking? It is important for you to be honest with yourself and God here.

Why is it alluring to join in a conversation containing those elements?

How can you best handle the next time you are tempted?

Let's go to the opposite circumstance—the temptation to share confidential information in order to defend someone. Why is the temptation to open our mouths here so strong?

When you're in a conversation with people who expect that you have knowledge about the situation or person being discussed, but you don't say a word—either to acquit or condemn—people observe that you can keep a confidence and aren't a blabbermouth. By your silence they learn your character.

One last area of character to discuss today is keeping our word. We reveal excellence in what we do by doing what we say we will do. This is another reason to say no to what is not from God. The thing that doesn't fit is the thing we end up looking for an excuse not to do. When we finally find a flimsy excuse not to do it, we renege. That puts a dent in our integrity. When was the last time you said you would do something but didn't follow through?

Would your friends, family, or coworkers say this is a habit with you?

Read Matthew 21:28-32. In this parable which son does Jesus criticize? Why?

What is the main reason you don't keep your word?

What can you do to change that?

We need to be attentive to the areas of our lives that seem insignificant but speak loudly to our character and testimony. If you aren't called to do something or don't want to do it, say no.

Finally today, we will talk about dressing like princesses to honor our Lord. What we wear—our style—instantly speaks more about us than we can say in an hour of conversation. Our youngest daughter, Kerry, is a high school freshman. Some mornings she announces at breakfast, "This is my I'm-tired-and-don't-want-to-try-to-look-cute-today outfit." What does your outfit today say about you?

In Proverbs 31 we have a role model in the "wife of noble character" (v. 10). One of her characteristics is that she is "clothed in fine linen and purple" (v. 22). Verse 24 says, "She makes linen garments and sells them." However, in these verses two different words for *linen* are used. In verse 22 the word used means "white linen" or "fine . . . linen" or "silk."[57] In verse 24 the word used means "to envelop; a wrapper" or "sheet."[58] What distinction do you see in what the Proverbs 31 woman wears and what she sells?

I don't understand this to mean we are to buy the most expensive clothes we can find, but that we should dress nicely within our budget. Verse 11 states, "Her husband has full confidence in her." If she were spending the rent money on clothes, I doubt her husband would have full confidence in her. What does verse 23 say about this woman's husband?

What does verse 30 say about the intentions of her heart?

This woman is not focused on vanity—trying to look like she's thirty when she's forty or even older. She wants to look her best, honoring her husband and her Lord.

Now we come to what might be the most sensitive subject in this book. It could seem frivolous, but how we present ourselves cuts to the core of who we are, who we are trying to hide from others, and who we want to be. Remind yourself of who you are (meditate on what you have written in Royal Truths). Who, what, or why are you trying to hide from others? Admit this to the Lord, and write it down. You may want to talk with someone if this answer has an ugly face that you don't know how to deal with.

Who are you trying to portray to others, your royal princess self or a facade?

✦ ✦ ✦ ✦ ✦ ✦ ✦ ✦ ✦ ✦ ✦

DAY FOUR: Pursue It!

It's been a busy, hard week. Take a minute and soak in your relationship with your Father. Go to the Royal Truths and linger over God's character and who you are in Christ. Feel the love of God smiling on you.

Once again I must ask you—is or has God been stirring you? If not, that's fine. Pursue relationship with your Father, the King. If he is stirring you, what are you doing in obedience to what he is showing you?

In Acts 10 we see God perfectly illustrate obedience in two men's stories. Read Acts 10. In verses 4-6 what did the angel tell Cornelius to do?

How did Cornelius respond (vv. 7, 8)?

In verses 9-16 what was happening with Peter?

While Peter was still pondering the vision, what happened? And how did Peter respond (vv. 17-23)?

Looking at the rest of Acts 10, what were the results of these two men obeying the vision God gave them? How were Cornelius and his family affected?

What about Peter?

We never know what will come from our obedience to doing the next thing God puts in front of us. I am working my way through the Old Testament. At first I was bogged down with so many details given to the Israelites on how to offer sacrifices, live righteously, and worship . . . not to mention the genealogies. Then God gently showed me that all these details revealed a part of his character—God is in the details. So what seems to be a small thing to me is a vital part of his plan. God's economy has no small details.

Read Matthew 25:14-30. How many talents did each man have entrusted to him, and what did each man do with his talents?

How did the master respond to the man given one talent?

Fill in the rest of the master's commendation to the first two servants: "Well done, good and faithful servant! You have been _____ ; I will put you _____ . Come and share your master's happiness!" What did the first two servants do to receive this response?

What did the third servant do to receive his response?

Can you remember an opportunity you passed up, even though you were gifted to do it, because you felt it was too unimportant to consider? Describe the details.

What will be your response the next time God brings an opportunity to you that fits your gifting, passion, and priorities?

Seeing God's hand in what he brings our way is so important. When God called me to my dream, I had a specific goal in mind, and I felt it was from God. That goal might still be something God has for me. But I am amazed both at the journey and at the most unexpected stops along the way. Opportunities have come that I never could have imagined—different, unique, and surprising. Yes, God and I are on this trip together. He has the map and the sites of interest along the way. I'm in the passenger's seat. When he says, "We have a point of interest coming up," I'm ready to jump out and experience the next adventure.

That's why being in God's timing is important as we pursue our dreams. We don't want to sit when God says go, but we definitely don't want to run ahead of God.

In the Bible we see many examples of people who weren't ready and willing when God told them to move. Gideon (Judges 6–8) was hiding out from the enemy when God called him to "save Israel out of Midian's hand" (6:14). In your own words, what did God tell Gideon in the last sentence of verse 14?

Peter is a good example of someone rushing ahead of God. Jesus chose Peter, James, and John to join him at the top of a mountain for one-time-only event (Mark 9:2-8). Jesus "was transfigured before them. His clothes became dazzling white, whiter than anyone in the world could bleach them. And there appeared before them Elijah and Moses, who were talking with Jesus." I don't know about you, but this experience would send me to the ground on my face, shaking and speechless. But not Peter. What was Peter's response?

How did God respond to Peter's suggestion?

God knows what we don't know we don't know. He knows our tendency to rely on what we see. That's why he teaches us over and over to listen to him and obey. God may have given you a glimpse of where he is taking you, but you need to wait on his direction because you don't know the whole plan.

Finally, let's look at a man who believed what God showed him to do and trusted God for the timing. Caleb was one of the spies included in the group sent by Moses to check out Canaan, the promised land. He went with eleven other men. Read Numbers 13:21-33. What kind of report did the other men give to Moses, Aaron, and the Israelites?

What report did Caleb give?

How did the other men respond to that? What does this reveal about their faith in what God had told them of his plan for them?

Numbers 14 tells a fabulous story of men of faith, as well as the tragic results of doubting and disobeying God. From verses 22, 23, 29-35, 37, and 38, what were the consequences of disbelief?

How did God describe Caleb (v. 24)?

What did God promise Caleb and Joshua (vv. 24, 30)?

We will have corresponding consequences for our responses to God's call.

One More Thing

Throughout this book we have talked about the temptation to compare ourselves and our lives with other people and their experiences. The same danger exists when we compare our callings and the timing of our callings with those of others. Turn to John 21:21, 22. How does Jesus answer us when we ask, "What about her?"

He says this because he loves you and he knows his plan for you is best!

Looking Back

How did the week go? How do you now define success? Add it to your Royal Truths. In your mind, have you been processing your priorities? List those in the Royals Truths too. (Don't worry—it's only paper. If God redirects you, you can rewrite them.)

Wow, princess! You are doing great. I know this is a spiritual workout, but it is worth it!

chapter eight

Principles for Your Journey to Fabulous

The Princess Learns
Her Royal Life Takes Discipline

"Princess, time to start your day!" chirped the lady-in-waiting.

"I don't want to. I want to sleep longer," came Jessica's pouty reply. Weeks of training had tired her.

The King passed Jessica's partially open door in time to overhear. He stepped in. "Jessica," he said sternly, "you are a real princess, not a fairy-tale princess. You have work to do."

Princess Jessica shot up in bed. "But . . . Father, I *have* been working. I need a day off."

"Get dressed," the King instructed, "and meet me in the east turret." He left before she could protest.

Jessica climbed the winding staircase to the top of the turret, all the while wondering what this was all about.

"Good morning again, Jessica."

"Father, why are we meeting here?" asked Jessica.

"I want you to survey the scene around and below us and tell me what you see."

"I see the kingdom, Father."

"Based on what you see, what is your first priority in helping me rule the kingdom?"

"Me? Help you rule? But . . . but I'm the youngest! Father, I don't know where to begin."

"Exactly. You must learn two principles—the Principle of Neglect and the Principle of Blinders. You must learn what is important and what can wait."

Princess Jessica thought for a few moments. Then she said, "Father, answer me one question."

"Anything, dear child."

"Must we learn this lesson so early in the morning?" she teased.

The King chuckled. "That is your first lesson of the day. Princesses must persevere. Being a princess takes discipline. Rising early and working hard will teach you that discipline."

✦ ✦ ✦ ✦ ✦ ✦ ✦ ✦ ✦ ✦ ✦

Life is getting exciting for Princess Jessica, and I hope for you too. Your rich, abundant life promised by Jesus is in view, but you have work to do.

We can still learn lessons from Moses, Caleb, and the Israelites. Let's go back to Numbers 13, 14. As you remember, in Numbers 13 the Israelites camped near the promised land, ready to take possession of it. God instructed Moses, "Send out men to explore the land of Canaan, the land I am giving to the Israelites" (13:2, *NLT*). The spies were not to determine whether the land could be taken. Their job was to gather facts regarding the land so Moses and the leadership could assess what they were up against. God had promised this land to his people. Israel would need to fight to possess it, however, and that would take discipline. If we are going to live out the dream God has given us, we need to be disciplined too.

Hard Work

Hard and *work* are two words most of us don't like to see together, especially if they are referring to us! Sure, we don't mind working hard, but hard work as a lifestyle is . . . well, hard work. But nothing in life of value or substance is attained without hard work.

My family and I watched the TV coverage of the summer Olympics in Beijing. I enjoyed the stories about the journeys of the athletes to qualify for the Olympics. Each athlete's story included hard work, dedication, and sacrifice. Our dreams will be accomplished with these same elements. However, unlike at the Olympics, *everyone* working in God's kingdom has the opportunity to earn "medals." Our work has eternal value and will never be forgotten by the King. "God is not unjust; he will not forget your work and the love you have shown him as you have helped his people and continue to help them" (Hebrews 6:10).

The woman of Proverbs 31:10-31 is an excellent role model for the discipline of hard work. I count ten verses in that passage that talk about her hard work. She did not goof off. She was serious about the mission God gave her. "She . . . works with eager hands. . . . She gets up while it is still dark; she provides food for her family and portions for her servant girls. . . . She sets about her work vigorously. . . . Her lamp does not go out at night" (vv. 13, 15, 17, 18). If you want to complete the mission God gave you, you will need to adopt her work ethic.

Many times people ask me how to get started in writing or how to get their work published. I am thrilled to share with them what I know; however, in the publishing world instant success is rare. Writing is a ton of hard work and takes lots of time, not only to write but also to see results. When I share these unglamorous realities, I immediately sense who is serious and dedicated. The dedicated writer has a sober look but an attitude of acceptance; I can see her thinking, *OK, I will do this.* The not-so-dedicated writer dismisses my comments as not pertinent to her. (That is OK; I offered what I knew to be truth.)

God speaks honorably about his people who work hard for him:

+ "The men in charge of the renovation worked hard and made steady progress. They restored the Temple of God according to its original design and strengthened it" (2 Chronicles 24:13, *NLT*).
+ "I put Shelemiah the priest, Zadok the scribe, and a Levite named Pedaiah in charge of the storerooms. I made Hanan son of Zaccur, the son of Mattaniah, their right-hand man. These men had a reputation for honesty and hard work" (Nehemiah 13:13, *The Message*).
+ "Mordecai the Jew ranked second in command to King Xerxes. He was popular among the Jews and greatly respected by them. He worked hard for the good of his people; he cared for the peace and prosperity of his race" (Esther 10:3, *The Message*).
+ "Dear brothers and sisters, honor those who are your leaders in the Lord's work. They work hard among you and give you spiritual guidance" (1 Thessalonians 5:12, *NLT*).

I want to be a hard worker for God. He is the almighty, living God, and he loves me. This is the least I can do for him. God's Word gives us many great examples of hard workers. Here are just four:

- The Israelite craftsmen used their skills to build the tabernacle (Exodus 36–39).
- Jacob shepherded for his father-in-law for fourteen years to earn his beloved Rachel (Genesis 29).
- The prophets Isaiah, Jeremiah, and Ezekiel prophesied in written and oral word and sometimes with actions to an unrepentant people.
- The apostle John wrote in the book of Revelation what Jesus told him and the amazing and sometimes graphic scenes Jesus showed him. Experiencing these scenes and writing about them undoubtedly had to be exhausting work.

What about you? Will God note you as one of his faithful who worked hard at her mission? Your calling is not a hobby to tinker with when you have time; it's a mission from God you must work to accomplish. My friend Anne has a singing and speaking ministry. She followed God's direction to make a CD. I had no idea the hours needed to record, rerecord, edit, and mix a CD! Anne worked diligently for months, and today she gave me one of her beautiful CDs. Listening to it made my spirit soar. Her hard work is now paying off.

Perseverance

Hard work must be in partnership with perseverance to attain success. This is true in your walk with the Lord, your relationships, your job, your parenting, and your calling. If you give your best only part of the time, your life will be like a puzzle with half the pieces missing. The picture looks promising and interesting, but without all the pieces it is incomplete and not worth much.

Perseverance keeps us going when we want to quit or take a break. Taking time off is good and necessary, but we can't just stop whenever we feel like it. We must wait until the time is right. Our friends' son, Matthew, met the woman of his dreams, Chloe. They planned to get married, but Matthew is in medical school and had only a small window of time off. During that short break, they celebrated a fabulous wedding. Now he is back in school. Both he and his bride plan for the day when they can take their careers as doctor and teacher to minister in a country closed to Christianity. Matthew and Chloe persevere toward their God-given mission.

One of the most influential people in my writing career is Bob Hostetler, an accomplished author. His class was my favorite at a writing conference I attended. At the beginning of the class, he made this statement: "There are two kinds of authors—the hobbyist and the professional. You must decide which one you are." You must make a similar decision. I will rephrase it for you: "There are two kinds of princesses—the princess unaware and the strong, confident princess. You must decide which one you will be." The princess unaware drifts wherever life takes her. Even if she has accepted Christ, she does not listen to God and his plan for her. She lives clueless, fearful . . . making excuses for anything that might stretch her or cause her to break a nail.

But the strong, confident princess boldly rides her Father's regal steed, holding on tight as he breaks into a full canter, the wind blowing in her face. She knows her life is about more than her. She wants to live every moment of it with purpose and excellence. Risk taking is just another part of her day. The life of the strong, confident princess takes perseverance.

I don't believe we know what we are signing on for when we say yes to God's call. I didn't. God knew that; so many times before we got started, he brought me to a point of affirming to him my commitment. One of those times is forever fresh in my memory. Our church had invited a special speaker to preach. I don't remember his name. He spoke on Colossians 4:7-18. I don't remember the subject of his message! However, as he closed his sermon, he read verse 17: "Tell Archippus: 'See to it that you complete the work you have received in the Lord.'"

When the speaker read those words out of holy Scripture, I knew God was speaking them directly to me. At the bottom of the page in my Bible, I wrote, "The Mom Book. 6-13-04. God spoke to me in church and took my breath away. I will, Lord." By now you know I'm a practical, living-by-truth girl. If a wave of emotion sweeps through a room, I'm the woman *not* crying. So when God took my breath away, he did so to make sure I knew he'd spoken to me. He wanted me to persevere with the book idea he had given me. He knew it would be a long process and a lot of hard work.

More than one year later, in December 2005, I signed the contract for *Queen Mom*. It was released in April 2007, almost three years from the time I wrote that note. Perseverance.

The Principle of Neglect

The next principle crucial to my mission is the Principle of Neglect—put first things first; that is, neglect until later the things that can wait. And neglect altogether those things that don't matter or are not yours to deal with. Let's dissect and examine this principle.

First, put first things first. This is another reason we need to know our priorities—so we know what is first for us. I am the kind of woman who likes to get the house in order first thing in the morning—do the dishes, start the laundry, pick up clutter. I also like to do my exercising before eight (I heard your whiny ugh!). It's the way God wired me. However, after I get all this done it is easily ten—half the morning is over. And oh, I am a morning person (I heard another ugh!), so my late nights are for sleeping. But my best time to write is morning through early afternoon. When I apply the Principle of Neglect, my day looks something like this: I spend time with Kerry at breakfast. After she is on the bus, I head to the computer. Breakfast dishes sit on the counter and the bed stays unmade. I try to squeeze in a power walk later in the day. I write till my brain overheats—usually early afternoon. Then I shift into overdrive and attack my household chores. I have everything done by the time the family starts coming in the door.

Do you see how I put off what could wait until after I accomplished my most important chore for the day—writing my daily word count? Yes, my relationships with God and my family come before my ministry—I start my day with God before my family gets up. When my family is home, I am available and interacting with them. The secondary chores were easily done after my writing. I gave my best time of day to my ministry.

I don't give you these specific details for you to compare yourself to me; I do it to put some meat on the bones. I want to help you apply this principle to your life by seeing what it looks like in mine.

Another writer I know and admire attacks his calling in a different way. He is a doctor with a young family. His days are filled with patients and his evenings with his wife and sons. However, he works well at night, so after the boys are tucked into bed, he works on his latest novel. This process works well for him and his family. He could fritter away his evenings watching *Lost*, but he knows he is set apart by God to write. First things first.

Finally, in the Principle of Neglect we must be wise enough to know what doesn't matter and what is not ours to deal with. Then we need to be strong enough to delete those things from our radar screen. They are a distraction.

Jesus practiced the Principle of Neglect. In Matthew 12:46-50 we see Jesus putting first things first. Mary and Jesus' half brothers came while he was teaching in the midst of a crowd. Word got to Jesus that they wanted to talk to him. Jesus responded, "Who is My mother and who are My brothers?" (v. 48, *NASB*). Then he motioned toward the disciples and said, "Behold My mother and My brothers! For whoever does the will of My Father who is in heaven, he is My brother and sister and mother" (vv. 49, 50, *NASB*).

These words of Jesus are some of his hard teachings. Matthew Henry explains, "His mother and brethren stood without, desiring to speak with him, when they should have been standing within, desiring to hear him. . . . They not only would not hear him themselves, but they interrupted others that *heard him gladly*." He adds, "Not that natural affection is to be put off, or that, under pretence of religion, we may be disrespectful to parents, or unkind to other relations; but *every thing is beautiful in its season*, and the less duty must stand by, while the greater is done."[59] Matthew Henry makes a great point. Jesus was not neglecting his family. He knew that what they needed could wait and was a distraction from God's immediate plan for him.

Jesus' later actions complete the teaching. Jesus was hanging on the cross, in pain not only from the crucifixion itself but also from the barbaric torture he had endured beforehand. Through all his pain and suffering, he thought of his mother, Mary, and lovingly enacted his final responsibility to her and provided for her future: "When Jesus saw his mother there, and the disciple whom he loved standing nearby, he said to his mother, 'Dear woman, here is your son,' and to the disciple, 'Here is your mother.' From that time on, this disciple took her into his home" (John 19:26, 27). As the oldest son, Jesus was responsible for his mother. This was a time when Mary needed Jesus. He cared for her by providing a loving home where she would be protected after his death.

Whatever the issue that brought Mary and the brothers to Jesus in Matthew 12 obviously wasn't something on Jesus' priority list. Jesus understood his ministry. If this had been on his priority list, he would have known it and done it. Since it wasn't his, he applied the Principle of Neglect. Jesus followed the Principle of Neglect by realizing what was his to do and what was not his to do.

We too need to be wise and discerning about what is ours and what is not. The strong, confident princess will catch the attention of those around her—at work, at church, and in charitable organizations. People will start thinking, *She is a sharp woman with a lot to offer. We could use someone like her.* And the opportunities will start flooding in. We need to know what is not ours to deal with.

The Principle of Neglect can be applied in varying degrees, depending on the intensity of the current project. When I am working on a deadline, I am dedicated to my writing schedule. When the deadline is met and I am working on editing and other ministry work, I adjust my schedule, allowing time for exercise and the occasional lunch with a friend. However, I still run my decisions and schedule through the Principle of Neglect, making adjustments as necessary.

Some of us spend our time on details that slow us down and don't matter for eternity. A clean house is honoring to the Lord; however, I once heard of someone who washes the inside of the toilet tank. Hmm. I'm thinking it's OK to neglect this detail.

The Principle of Blinders

The last discipline we will discuss is the Principle of Blinders. Most of us are familiar with the blinders a horse wears to keep his eyes focused directly in front of him. The jockey puts these on his racehorse so the horse won't be distracted by other horses. As a result, the horse's focus is the finish line and nothing else. A carriage driver in a busy city puts blinders on his horse so the horse won't be distracted or frightened by traffic or crowds. The horse's focus is the street in front of him, not the chaos of taxis, cars, and buses.

We live in a world of many distractions—some exciting, some frightening, some interesting. But they all take our focus off our goal. To be successful and complete the mission God gave us, we need to put on blinders.

Peter got the point of the Principle of Blinders when Jesus sternly reprimanded him for looking at John and asking, "What about him?" Jesus pointedly told Peter, "You must follow me" (John 21:21, 22). Jesus knew that each of the apostles would have differing yet important ministries in starting the New Testament church. He knew each man would have to focus on his mission in order to accomplish it. Looking around, comparing missions, wondering why the other guy got to do this or that would cause the apostles to crash and burn. Other princesses might be doing lots of exciting, fun things or getting recognition for their hard work, but Jesus teaches us to keep our blinders on and keep our eyes on him.

My dear friend Kimberly is in full-time Christian ministry. She works out of her home, so it is easy for people to assume she is always available. However, that is not true. Kimberly is one of the most focused, disciplined people I know. She would be the first to tell you that this is not natural to her but something God is working into her character. Recently Kimberly shared with me how once again she kept her focus on the goal God had given her. She was nearing completion on a project with a pressing deadline when a friend called and invited her out for a day of fun. Kimberly graciously said that she needed to finish her project. Her friend did not relent; she did not understand Kimberly's call from God or the Principle of Blinders. To successfully do the mission God had given her, Kimberly needed to stay home, work, and persevere, which she did. When we say no, and many times we must, we risk being misunderstood.

Let's reread John 7:1-10. Remember that Jesus' brothers were less than supportive of his ministry. The brothers mocked Jesus: "You ought to leave here and go to Judea, so that your disciples may see the miracles you do. . . . Show yourself to the world" (vv. 3, 4). Jesus told them, "The right time for me has not yet come" (v. 6). Jesus told them no and was misunderstood. Are we willing to risk being misunderstood for following our Lord?

Jesus' life was full of misunderstandings. In the community's view, Jesus' birth was illegitimate. He lived a perfect life, so what better fodder for gossip? What was he up to anyway? He said he came to save the Jews but refused to let them make him king. If he was planning to rule, why pick the working class as followers? Why not go to the educated and choose the brightest? He said he was the Messiah, but he died at the hands of the Romans. Jesus' life and mission were a puzzle to many, and many wrote him off as a misguided, well-meaning man. But Jesus knew the truth—correction, Jesus *is* the truth (John 14:6). He lived the life he was sent to live, and he let those who chose to, misunderstand him.

In the 2008 presidential election, Senator John McCain chose Sarah Palin, governor of Alaska, to be his running mate. Just days after the announcement, the news broke that Governor Palin's seventeen-year-old daughter was five months pregnant. The press tried to stir up controversy, and Governor Palin and her husband, Todd, issued a statement: "Our beautiful daughter Bristol came to us with news that as parents we knew would make her grow up faster than we had ever planned. We're proud of Bristol's decision to have her baby and even prouder to become grandparents. . . . Bristol and the young man she will marry are going to realize very quickly the difficulties of raising a child, which is why they will have the love and support of our entire family."[60] The Palin family was totally misunderstood by the media. Like so many of us, they do their best to walk with the Lord, live out their values, and raise their children accordingly. However, life does not always go as planned. I deeply admire Sarah Palin and her family for persevering in the vision God gave them—public service—while walking with him and making right choices in difficult circumstances. Being misunderstood for following God is hard.

The benefit of the Principle of Blinders is satisfaction in a job well done. My friend Kimberly summed up her Principle of Blinders experience: "It is deep-soul satisfying. It is never easy and always requires perseverance. It will require incredible sacrifice and discipline. But then we know it's God." The strong, confident princess commits to the disciplines that will take her on her Father's journey and to his destination.

When we are living the life of discipline for God, we will feel a certain amount of isolation—of being called apart by God. Recently I was privileged to have lunch with a small group of women who are all leaders in women's ministry. We were asked to tell a bit of our experience. Many of us shared the same theme—being called by God to a place of isolation. We are not locked up and refusing to go out, but God lessened the time we spent with friends. He has guided us to go to him first before calling a friend. We were not whining or feeling sorry for ourselves. On the contrary, we shared a depth of relationship with God that we could not have learned otherwise. You too may find yourself being pulled by God to a place of aloneness with him. But you are not really alone. God is with you, and millions of other princesses are in the same fabulous experience.

Finding the Fabulous

We have another exciting week of walking with the Lord ahead of us! I hope you are feeling the freedom and exhilaration that come with being the princess instead of trying to conform to someone else's expectations.

Looking Ahead

This week think about your strengths in the disciplines we are studying. Think too about a discipline that might be new to you or that you need to practice.

✦ ✦ ✦ ✦ ✦ ✦ ✦ ✦ ✦ ✦ ✦

DAY ONE: Princesses Must Work Too

The Proverbs 31 woman is a princess to learn from. Read Proverbs 31:10-31. List the phrases and corresponding verses that describe her work or her attitude toward her work.

Don't be overwhelmed. She did not do all these tasks in one day! She is a role model.

The rest of the Bible also sets out models and goals for us, but God understands that we will not be perfect until we meet Jesus in Heaven.

We have been discussing who we are and defining what our lives will be about from this point forward. Who would the woman in Proverbs 31 say she is, and what would she say her life is about?

In this chapter and chapter 7, we discussed how we will live with excellence the life God planned for us. How did the woman in Proverbs 31 do that (vv. 13, 15, 17, 18, 25-27)?

Again, accurate Bible study requires considering the whole teaching of the Word. So while it looks as if this Proverbs 31 princess never took a break, let's also consider the life of Jesus. He pulled away from ministry for time with his Father and fun with his friends. The rich life God has for us is balanced. Our attitude is key—we are about God's business. Sometimes that means working hard, and sometimes it means swinging in the hammock with a good book.

If you came to me and asked how to achieve the vision God gave you, I would tell you everything we have discussed in chapters 7 and 8. What would be your reaction? Would you embrace the principles, or would you say, "Brenda may have to do those things, but I know that an easier way will also work"?

God honors those who work hard for him. List the phrase in the following verses that states God's commendation.

2 Chronicles 24:13

Nehemiah 13:13

Esther 10:3

1 Thessalonians 5:12

You want God to refer to you with similar words. What good habits and attitudes do you currently have that would group you with the previous descriptions?

What habits or attitudes do you need to drop?

We have discussed using our spiritual gifts and talents in our callings. Now I want to put some meat on those bones so we have a better understanding of working hard with our gifts and talents.

> Then the LORD said to Moses, "Look, I have specifically chosen Bezalel son of Uri, grandson of Hur, of the tribe of Judah. I have filled him with the Spirit of God, giving him great wisdom, ability, and expertise in all kinds of crafts. He is a master craftsman, expert in working with gold, silver, and bronze. He is skilled in engraving and mounting gemstones and in carving wood. He is a master at every craft!
>
> "And I have personally appointed Oholiab son of Ahisamach, of the tribe of Dan, to be his assistant. Moreover, I have given special skill to all the gifted craftsmen so they can make all the things I have commanded you to make" (Exodus 31:1-6, *NLT*).

In these verses God gave two men their mission. What were Bezalel's spiritual gifts? How do you know?

What were his talents?

Oholiab's "special skill" to "make all the things [God had] commanded" was a unique gifting from God, his spiritual gift. Oholiab's talent was his craftmanship. He knew his way around the tools and materials. God enabled him to make the sacred items for Israel's worship. An overview of Exodus 25–40 (don't worry, I'm not going to make this part of the assignment!) shows the detail for each piece of the tabernacle and the tabernacle itself. These men had extensive and detailed hard work to do; it would not be done overnight. They committed themselves to work hard using their spiritual gifts and talents to complete their mission from God.

Think About It

Do you have the attitude of a hard worker? Even if you are not sure where God is calling you, does your daily life reflect character that is eager to work and complete the task? Describe your struggles and your strengths.

✦ ✦ ✦ ✦ ✦ ✦ ✦ ✦ ✦ ✦ ✦

DAY TWO: Princess Perseverance

Perseverance is the one discipline that will push us over the finish line. Kelsey and I watched on TV as Constantina Tomescu-Dita won the women's 2008 Olympic marathon in Beijing.[61] It was excruciating to watch. I can only imagine the perseverance it took for her not only to finish but also to win the marathon. Describe a time when you persevered past what you thought you were capable of.

The key to perseverance is motivation. Constantina won a gold medal and a line in the record books. I don't know if that was her only motivation; I'm sure it went much deeper.

So what is my motivation? Let's look at what God says should motivate us. Read Hebrews 12:1-3. In verse 1 what are we instructed to do?

What hinders or encumbers you as you persevere in your race?

What is your entangling sin?

A hindrance may seem innocent, but it gets us off track. It might be an issue needing to be pruned from your life. You try to move ahead with God, but this issue or activity or person keeps tripping you up and distracting you. An entangling sin is just that—a sin that we fall for time and time again, that wraps itself around us, keeping us prisoner. We feel we will never be worthy to serve God, because we are forever falling for this sin.

In verses 2, 3, what hard things did Jesus experience?

What was his motivation?

In contemplating Jesus as our perfect example, what is our motivation?

In light of what Jesus went through, his motivation, and our motivation, what will you do with the hindrance in your life?

What about your entangling sin? Commit to getting out from under it. If the hold it has on you is getting tighter, you may want to ask a mature Christian woman to pray with you and advise you. You may want to seek professional Christian counsel. Remember, this is yours to deal with. Jesus is with you and will help you, but no one else can do it for you.

When we are in the midst of working hard, it is easy to focus on the wrong motivation. Read Galatians 2:11-21. Why was Peter in trouble with Paul?

Jesus' mission was to bring the new covenant to man. This means believers no longer need to follow all the rules of the old covenant in order to be right with God. Jesus is our righteousness before God. One of the old rules was that Jews were to be circumcised. Traditionally, Gentiles were not and were considered unclean. Jews were not allowed to eat with Gentiles. In the new covenant we are all one in Christ (Romans 10:12). In Galatians 2 Peter had stopped eating with the Gentile believers "because he was afraid of those who belonged to the circumcision group" (v. 12). Peter wanted to please the Jews. Wrong motivation! Paul called him on it.

So what is my motivation? I want to be able to stand before God and hand him my best and see a smile on his face. When Bob Hostetler challenged a classroom full of fledgling writers to decide which they were—hobbyist or professional—I instantly said, "Professional!" That was a time of decision, commitment, and affirmation to

God. I heard him and was answering his call. My motivation also includes sharing the truth of God's Word with women who, like me, desperately need it. I want women to know God, his peace, and his pleasure in us.

Princess Unaware, what is your motivation? What drives you? Does your motivation need to change? If yes, what changes do you need to make?

Another key component of perseverance is focusing on truth. The enemy is the father of lies (John 8:44). He will do whatever he can to sneak his lies into your thoughts and cause you to doubt the vision God gave you, to doubt the gifts God gave you, and especially to doubt that God is with you 100 percent—and 100 percent of the time. Continue to write on index cards the verses that speak to you, and keep them with you. Meditate on them. God's Word sends the enemy running.

What truth do you need to remember today? Start with your Royal Truths. Review who God is and how much he loves you. Review who you are—no longer a peasant but a princess of the King. What has God called you to do? (Also write your response in the Royal Truths; it is a truth from God).

Know that when you are seeking God, growing in relationship with God, and doing what God made you to do in his timing, you are in the center of God's will, the safest place to be.

The next truth we need to know and memorize is one I put on the first page of my book of index cards. Read Joshua 1:5. I love the wording in the *NASB*: "I will not fail you or forsake you." God also reassures us of this fact in Deuteronomy 31:6 and Hebrews 13:5. Remember, God's character cannot change. When God says, "I will not fail you or forsake you," you know he means forever and ever. Add this truth about God to your Royal Truths. How will this truth affect you the next time you want to quit or doubt that God is in this crazy dream?

When I get tired or don't think I can keep going, I am refreshed by Psalm 138:8: "The Lord will accomplish what concerns me; your lovingkindness, O Lord, is everlasting; do not forsake the works of Your hands" (*NASB*). God will accomplish the plan he has for me. It's not all me. It's God. Just as Israel had to fight for the promised land, we need to work for our vision, but the power and the results are from God.

Journey back with me to June 13, 2004. Sit next to me in the church pew and listen as the guest speaker reads Colossians 4:17: "Tell Archippus: 'See to it that you complete the work you have received in the Lord.'" Hear the Lord encouraging you personally: "Tell _____ (your name): 'See to it that she completes the work she has received in the Lord.'" Your life—your vision, job, family, ministry—it's all work you have received from God. He gave it to you, and he will empower you to finish it. If you believe this, put your name in the above blank and date it. One more step completed in becoming the strong, confident princess!

✦ ✦ ✦ ✦ ✦ ✦ ✦ ✦ ✦ ✦ ✦

DAY THREE: The Princess Practices Neglect

The Principle of Neglect creates space in our lives for us to do the important things God gives us to do. It shoves to the side the pesky creatures that try to steal our time, energy, money, and talents—all meant to be used for God. The Principle of Neglect forces us to choose the best over the good and the bad. Our priorities should list what is our best. Review your priorities from the Royals Truths. Now list them below.

These are the pieces of your life God wants you to be devoted to. Create a strategy to live out these priorities and accomplish your mission from God by listing the top three priorities in your day. Be brutal, and no excuses.

I trust you were tough and didn't shrink back. We will never accomplish God's plan for us if we keep giving in to people or activities that siphon off our best. Give these top three the best time slots you have. What is the best time to perform them? List them again with their time allocations.

Now fit what remains on your list into the remaining time in your day. And please give yourself time for adequate sleep and refreshment. The intention is not for you to have every minute of the day stuffed. This is your Principle of Neglect plan:

Think through your day today or yesterday or one day last week. What clutter is in your day, things that don't matter whether you do them or not? Could these be delegated or dropped altogether?

Maybe some of this clutter is not yours at all. Maybe it belongs to someone else and you are being an enabler by trying to do it for him or her. If it's not on your priority list, it's not yours. (Don't start doubting your priorities. Remember, you prayed and sat at the feet of the Lord to hear his plan for you.) This may be an issue left over from pruning, and now is the time to deal with it. Whatever the reason for the clutter, it is still clutter, and a perfect opportunity for you to practice the Principle of Neglect. List the clutter here.

Commit here to neglect it. Date your commitment.

Wow. How are you doing? Anyone hyperventilating? If you just committed to neglecting something or someone who has been stealing precious moments, energy, and resources from your life, it is a major spiritual milestone. I don't take it lightly and neither should you. If you are doing this study with a group, take a minute and share with another person in your group how you will live out the plan you have created—your Principle of Neglect. Write your plan in your Royals Truths.

The enemy won't take your commitment lightly either. He loves being able to distract you with frivolities or nuisances. It's not much work on his part, but it creates the desired goal—keeping you from accomplishing God's plan. You need to be ready to keep your plan in play.

Turn back to Matthew 12:46-50. This story perfectly illustrates how to defend God's purposes for us. When have you experienced a similar situation? You were busy doing what God called you to—a service, a career where you are making a difference for the kingdom, raising your family by biblical teaching—and someone (maybe an extended family member, maybe a friend, but someone with a pull on you) interrupted and wanted your attention. Describe what happened.

These verses do not reveal how Jesus interacted with his family; we only know he didn't immediately go out to talk with them. Turn again to John 7:1-10. Review how Jesus responded to his brothers' jibes.

Jesus spoke truth but didn't go into truth they could not/would not understand—that he is God's Son and he was listening for God's direction. He spoke an appropriate amount of truth with graciousness and love. He didn't put them down, but he didn't give in to make them happy. How will you handle the situation the next time something similar happens to you?

The strong, confident princess knows her priorities, lives her priorities, and defends her priorities with truth and graciousness.

✦ ✦ ✦ ✦ ✦ ✦ ✦ ✦ ✦ ✦ ✦

DAY FOUR: The Princess Puts on Blinders

I have claustrophobic tendencies, so the thought of putting on blinders is suffocating. But in the disciplines of life, it is freeing. When I am wearing the blinders given to me by my Father, the King, I have peace, a sense of purpose, and clarity of thought. I am not being distracted by the thousands of options that vie for my glance. Even glancing is distracting.

Read John 21:15-22. Imagine the spiritual high Peter must have been on. To do that fully, we need to go back to the last time he had seen Jesus. Read Luke 22:54-62. What was the last interaction between Peter and Jesus before Jesus' crucifixion (v. 61)?

How would you have felt if you were Peter?

This verse is worthy of a study of its own, but we must keep our blinders on and accomplish the mission for today's study.

Let's go back to John 21, which takes place during the forty days Jesus spent on earth after his resurrection and before his ascension into Heaven. Jesus appeared to the disciples as they were fishing. After they finished breakfast, Jesus took time with Peter to get him back on task. OK, *now* imagine Peter's spiritual high. Peter had just learned he was right with Jesus and that Jesus had an important ministry for him. What did he do (vv. 20, 21)?

He removed the blinders Jesus had just placed on his ministry. He saw John and became distracted by what John would be doing for Christ. Oh, we are much the same way! God has blessed us beyond anything we think we might deserve (I mean, with the privilege of serving him), and we lift the edge of the blinders and sneak a peek at our sister, diverting our attention to where it shouldn't be.

Jesus had strong words for Peter. Write verse 22 here.

These strong words are for us too. Why would we think we are any better than Peter? As we live out the Principle of Blinders, we are sticking close to the Lord and becoming more comfortable with his plan. The rest of the world is going its way, however, and that is contrary to God's way. We will inevitably be misunderstood. That does not bother some people (mostly men, I think!), but I find that women usually like to be understood. I deeply need for you to understand me, even if you don't agree with me. (That's not right, I know. But it is an issue I struggle with.)

Jesus endured misunderstanding throughout his life. Let's look also at a couple of women who endured misunderstanding. I can't think of any woman who was more misunderstood than Mary, the mother of Jesus. Pregnant but not married. Gave birth to someone who claimed to be the Messiah. Other children in the family didn't understand the whole virgin-birth-perfect-Son-of-God thing. Yeah, Mary endured being misunderstood.

A modern-day example is vice-presidential candidate Sarah Palin. She and her family chose to do the right thing in a hard situation. Which of us hasn't had judgment passed on us or our families? Yeah, Sarah Palin endured being misunderstood.

What about you? Describe a situation in which you were misunderstood for doing what God called you to do.

How are you now better prepared to accept being misunderstood and not bother about defending yourself?

God finally brought me to a place of understanding; I must sacrifice to him my need to be understood. It is so freeing not to have to make sure everyone understands me and my choices.

One More Thing

How do you feel about God calling you aside to a place where you are no longer distracted and you can know God better?

Will you go? You know what's next—yep—commit to it, sign it, date it.

Looking Back

How did the week go? What discipline really challenged you? If you had to choose one, what is the most significant change you will make from the ideas in this chapter?

You are doing great on your journey to the fabulous! I am so proud of you.

chapter nine

Slaying Dragons

The Princess Learns to Recognize and Deal with Opposition

The King informed Princess Jessica that she had completed her training and now needed time in battle to prove everything she had learned. He kissed her cheek, helped her onto her horse, and swatted the horse's backside.

"Be on alert at all times!" he called after her. "Your enemy won't appear as you expect him to."

Only an hour into her mission from the King, Jessica was lonely. Then deep in the forest, she was surprised and delighted to come upon her sister. She dismounted.

"Sarah, what are you doing here?"

"Jessica! Don't you know it's dangerous for you to be this far away from home? Turn around and go back to the castle."

"What are you talking about? Father sent me on a mission. He wouldn't send me if he didn't believe I was ready."

Sarah sighed. "Father is well intentioned, but he doesn't really understand your limitations. Go. Go home," persisted her sister.

"But I trust Father! I'm moving on," Jessica said stubbornly.

"No. I won't let you pass."

"I *will* pass."

The two sisters were still arguing when Sarah's gaze was drawn upward toward the sky behind Jessica. A flicker of terror flashed in Sarah's eyes, but then . . . she looked back at Jessica, and the strangest smile crossed her face. It wasn't a pleasant smile. Sarah stepped back and eased herself behind a tree.

Whoosh . . . whoosh . . . came a sound behind Jessica. She turned, instinctively drawing her sword. A brightly colored dragon was breaking though the forest canopy, negotiating his wide wings through the trees, his eyes keen on his human prey. Then he was above her, claws extended, his jaws wide and terrible.

It's the Glittering Green! Jessica realized with horror.

She ducked, dodging his claws, and thrust her sword, piercing his neck. With a screech of agony, the dragon swept on, maintaining flight but careening wildly through the trees, breaking limbs as he went.

Jessica, shocked and enraged, whirled around to Sarah. "Why? Why didn't you warn me?"

"Now you see," Sarah said, strangely calm. "Father expects too much of us. I'm the only one who understands this. The others . . . they train, they fight, they wear themselves out. I just want to keep you safe, sister." Sarah smiled sourly. "After all, you are his new favorite."

Jessica was deeply hurt by Sarah's lack of understanding, by her envy. But she couldn't let it slow her down. She mounted her steed, gave him a swat, and rode on.

The next morning Princess Jessica arose from her bedroll and pulled out a mirror. She was smoothing her wild curls when she was suddenly alarmed by what she saw in place of her reflection. Another dragon was looking back at her, breathing fireballs. She released the mirror as if it were a fire itself. What was that whispering sound coming from the mirror? Jessica drew closer to it. Lies and doubts hissed at her: *You will fail. You're only a peasant girl. Are you sure the King said you are a princess?*

Again her training engaged. Princess Jessica pulled out the appropriate weapon—her Father's book—and began to read.

What a shock! Like Princess Jessica, we believe that because we are living boldly—being all God created us to be—we will have nothing but victory and success. Oh no! Now we are a threat to the enemy, so he pours it on. And the opposition doesn't look like we thought it would.

You know you are a one-of-a-kind, cherished, chosen, loved princess of the King. You are getting to know your Father for who he truly is. You are making changes in order to live the rich life he planned for you. I am thrilled! But not everyone will feel this way. You may be surprised by who is with you and who resists.

You are likely to experience opposition from one or more of three distinct sources. The tricky part is that opposition can come without warning and from those we'd least expect.

The Dragon of Opposition from Friends and Family

Friends and family members might come to us with words of "wisdom and caution," but are those words from God? Many times they are not for our good but to try to get us to abandon our princess life. We don't want to end our relationship with these people, but we do need to slay the opposition they present to the life God has for us.

Family and friends liked you the way you were. You were in a hut that cozied up to theirs, and life was good. (You all might have been miserable, but at least you were *all* miserable together.) Now you have moved, and friends and family are thinking, *Who do you think you are to get a better life?* People who were leaning on you have fallen over like dominoes. You are causing them discomfort. They are used to knowing where to find you and what to expect from you. They knew they had a certain amount of control over you. All that has changed, and they are not happy. Because you have changed, they might need to change; and change is one part of life they want to avoid.

Your new way of living might shine light on regrets in their lives—dreams not pursued, sins lived with, poisonous relationships endured, fallacies hung onto and not traded for the truth. Regret stings. Many people are stuck in their regrets, and seeing you move on nags them about the possibilities they passed up.

You know that pursuing the dream God gave you is sometimes scary, hard work. For these reasons, many people do not pursue what God put in them. They sacrifice their calling so they can keep their sin. It doesn't make sense, but we have all been there and had to make the choice. Yes, it is sad. I mourn for those who miss their intended lives. What is sadder is that many times they don't want to see others pursue their dreams. Know this—you don't need to condemn them but to understand them and respond with grace instead. Don't take their negative comments personally. Pray for them, but don't let them discourage you. As I tell my girls when they are misunderstood or verbally attacked without cause, "This is more about them than you."

A vivid example of this scenario comes from the life of Peter. Jesus talked to his disciples about what would happen to him in the near future—his torture, death, and resurrection (Matthew 16:21-28). Peter couldn't accept this. He believed he knew best for Jesus and his ministry and said, "Never, Lord! . . . This shall never happen to you!" (v. 22). But Jesus called it like it was. He said to Peter, "Get behind me, Satan! You are a stumbling block to me; you do not have in mind the things of God, but the things of men" (v. 23).

When others try to get in the way or stop God's purpose for us, they are helping Satan's purpose, whether they realize it or not. They are a stumbling block to us— something that makes us fall, obstructs our way, and slows us down. They are not thinking along with God but about what *they* want.

A dear friend of mine will leave with her husband tomorrow for ministry in a country closed to Christianity. They will take their three adorable young children. My friend and I have been through much together; her friendship is priceless to me. This morning we met for our last cup of coffee and piece of chocolate cake. Yesterday in church I sobbed over her and the children (yes, I know in the last chapter I said I never cry), so today I decided to have a meaningful conversation with her. Our time was rich and precious. We talked about the difficulty of following God, of her struggle in taking her kids away from everything and almost everyone they know. We came back to the same truth—this ministry is God's will for their family. Not going would not make their lives better.

It has been a process for me to adjust to the reality of her leaving. I have wept more than once and in public. However, I couldn't be more excited for her and their adventure. I have told her so often. I will encourage her, e-mail her pictures, and write to her. I will be there for her even though she is thousands of miles away, because that is what we do for others on their journey with the King.

Pray and look for those who will encourage you and help you on your journey to the fabulous. Mary, the mother of Jesus, knew how important this kind of relationship would be. Right after Gabriel visited her and gave her the amazing news that she would be the mother of the Messiah, Mary went to spend time with the only other woman who could possibly understand what she was experiencing— Elizabeth. Elizabeth was the mother of John the Baptist. Her pregnancy was a miracle too, because she had been barren and was "well along in years" (Luke 1:7).

Luke 1:39-56 tells about their time together, encouraging each other and rejoicing over what God was doing in and through their lives. Pray for God to bring you an Elizabeth.

The Dragon in the Mirror

Princess Jessica thought she had dealt with all her opposition. She was shocked when opposition came from her own mirror. We face the same dragon. We gather up our "royalness" and prepare to take a nice look at ourselves in the mirror, only to have our beautiful reflection turn into a scary dragon breathing fireballs of lies, doubts, and excuses. We must slay this dragon before he disables us from fulfilling our mission.

Let's look again to our how-to-do-or-not-do-ministry disciple, Peter. This time we find Peter stepping out into a thrilling adventure with Jesus (Matthew 14:22-36). Jesus was walking on the water toward the disciples in their boat. Peter, full of faith, wanted a piece of this action: "Lord, if it's you, . . . tell me to come to you on the water" (v. 28). Jesus responded, "Come." Totally forgetting himself, Peter got down from the boat and started walking toward Jesus on the water! He was doing the impossible. Then he looked into the mirror. He saw the wind. He factored in who he was—a mere fisherman, no one special. He started sinking.

We do the same thing. We start listening to the mirror's whispers, and we are rendered useless. Let's discuss five fireballs of opposition that the dragon throws to stop us.

Perfectionism

Perfectionism must have everything perfect all the time. It cannot distinguish what is good enough for the situation. Perfectionism measures its self-worth by the "perfectness" of its work. My good friend Elizabeth observed, "The root of perfectionism is insecurity." Ouch. "Just wanting to do a good job" might be a cover-up for our insecurities; the motive behind our perfectionism is not to honor God but to keep others from thinking poorly of us. Isn't that pride? First Peter 5:5 tells us, "God opposes the proud but gives grace to the humble."

As a result of our need to have everything perfect, we do not stay in step with God. I think Martha struggled a little with perfectionism (Luke 10:38-42). Luke tells us that "Martha was distracted by all the preparations" (v. 40). Isn't that what perfectionism does? It distracts us from the Lord.

Procrastination

Procrastination is another fireball of opposition the dragon uses to disable us. Procrastination dresses in beautiful intentions, but it never rolls up its sleeves and gets to work; it always finds a reason to stay out of the action and not get dirty. Procrastination is easily distracted. It focuses on what is in front of it, whether or not that issue is important.

The Principle of Neglect and the Principle of Blinders extinguish the fireball of procrastination. Applying the Principle of Neglect enables us to neglect those pesky creatures procrastination shuffles onto our path. The Principle of Blinders focuses us on God's plan for us, not the million distractions whining for our attention.

Laziness

Another fireball of opposition many of us refuse to dodge is laziness. We take a direct hit and then say, "Well, it's just my nature to be laid-back." Laziness is from the enemy. Once again he has found a way to render you useless without causing you to sin in a way that would convict you or cause other believers to confront you.

God has much to say regarding laziness. One powerful verse is Jeremiah 48:10: "A curse on him who is lax in doing the Lord's work!" Being lazy and neglectful of our responsibilities doesn't honor God. Laziness can be a symptom of deeper issues. If this is the case, recognize it and get counsel. Please know that God does not want you to lose one more day to this attack from the enemy. It is not God's plan for you.

Status Quo

The next fireball of opposition the dragon lobs into our lives is acceptance of the status quo. Life is good enough; why shake it up with radical ideas? Everything in moderation, right? Let's not go overboard with this religion stuff.

How easy it is for those of us living in the United States to settle into the proverbial "fat and sassy" way of life! Our needs are easily met and then some. We go to church and Bible study without persecution. We can openly speak about God and Jesus without being thrown into prison or having our homes torched. Why would we want to mess with this comfy life?

Because we were not put on this earth to grow fat and sassy! We were put here to glorify God and to grow in relationship with him. Accomplishing our mission will require getting up out of the cushy status quo and allowing God to get us into training. It's time to lose that "fat" and change our "It's all about me!" attitude. God wants his princesses fit and prepared for their lives and missions. God wants you to be his—thinking his way, knowing him, obeying him, and focused on his purposes. You can't do that from a status-quo lounger.

Excuses

The final fireball of opposition is all the excuses we come up with not to proceed as princesses. And we are good at coming up with them and then convincing others that they are truth:

+ "I am not qualified to . . ."
+ "No one would want me to . . ."
+ "I would love to, but I'm too busy right now."
+ "I've got other things more important in my life."
+ Or we may stay silent but think, *If I say yes to God, I will have to let go of my secret sin.*

Our excuses provide safe distance between us and the amazing life God has for us. When we look at life through the filter of our excuses, all we see is risk or uncertainty. We don't see God's provision, power, and plan.

Jesus addressed excuses in Luke 9:59-62. He called a man to follow him, but the man first wanted to go and bury his father. Jesus said, "Let the dead bury their own dead, but you go and proclaim the kingdom of God" (v. 60). He wasn't teaching us not to care for our families but not to use them as an excuse to keep from following him.

Many times we use our families as an excuse: "My family needs me." Yes, they do. You are a vital part of their lives. However, you are not their lifeblood nor are they yours. We don't stop caring for our families when we follow God. We keep our families in God's perspective. He will always be with them. They are in his perfect care.

Back to Luke 9:60. Jesus identified the man's reason as an excuse and gave him his mission: "You go and proclaim the kingdom of God." Let those words of Jesus disintegrate your excuses. We are called to live as strong, confident princesses. No more wallowing in mucky excuses. Our Father has provided everything we need for a fabulous life. If we don't use it, we are wasting the riches Jesus died to give us.

Discouragement from the Enemy

Finally, the last place we will find opposition is straight from the enemy, who does all he can to discourage us. The dragon of discouragement can stop us in our tracks with the enemy barely lifting a finger. He only needs to whisper in our ears. I asked friends to share with me the lies they hear from the enemy. The list included these:

- *You can't.*
- *You will fail. This will not work.*
- *You're too much—too loud, too complicated, too needy.*
- *You're not enough—not smart enough, not pretty enough . . . not enough as a friend, a daughter, a wife, or a mother.*
- *Who do you think you are?*
- *You don't have much to show for all your years with Christ and in the Word. You're a poor excuse for a Christian.*

When the enemy whispers these lies to us, if we don't examine them against truth, it's as if we are standing in the boxing ring with him and letting him pound us over and over. Discouragement is effective because, like so many obstacles we've discussed in this book, it is not viewed as a sin. We are less likely to identify it as a temptation from the enemy.

The enemy has hit me with discouragement so many times, my spiritual back looks like someone used it for target practice. He only needs to attack me at my weak area and I drop, taking myself out of the game.

Discouragement puts our focus on lies. We feel too weak to think on God's truth.

Discouragement convinces us that God has deceived us. This was Satan's original maneuver: "Did God really say, 'You must not eat from any tree in the garden'?" (Genesis 3:1). *Did God really say . . . ?* We wouldn't say God lied, but maybe he's not as invested in us as we thought. Or maybe we misunderstood what he told us to do. We'd better go back to our seats before anyone notices us living on the edge for God.

Discouragement wedges itself between God and us. It blocks our view of God, interfering with our relationship with him. We feel lonely, isolated, and hopeless—right where the enemy wants us. He knows when we feel forgotten by God and when we see no hope or feel useless. No, we aren't campaigning for the devil, but we definitely aren't working for the kingdom.

Jesus knows the pain of this separation. "About the ninth hour Jesus cried out in a loud voice, *'Eloi, Eloi, lama sabachthani?'*—which means, 'My God, my God, why have you forsaken me?'" (Mathew 27:46). Jesus was separated from God when he took our sins at the cross. I don't understand what he experienced in that time, but I do know he did it for me. He did it so I will never be separated from God (Romans 8:31-39). This is the truth I cannot let go of: I am never separated from God or out of his thoughts.

Our weapon to extinguish discouragement is God's truth. God is for us. Write Romans 8:31 on an index card. Memorize it. Find another verse, one that directly addresses your weak spot, and write it on an index card too. Now you have two great weapons for slaying discouragement. When the enemy is pummeling you with discouragement, recall God's truth; then look up to God and ask him to help you act on it. Plan now what you will do the next time the dragon breathes discouragement down your neck.

Discouragement is never God talking to you! It is always the enemy. If you are going the wrong way, God will tell you—but not with whispers of discouragement. God will speak to you in his strong, loving voice. He will speak to you through his Word. He will never belittle you, shame you, or taunt you—that is always the enemy. Throughout our journey to the fabulous, you have gotten to know your Father better. You know his voice. Trust his loving voice. Any other voice is from the enemy.

Princess Unaware, we must understand and accept these truths. We are God's princesses. He purposed us for victorious living—not to be puppets on a string for the enemy to jerk around at his whim. Take these truths and own them. Live them. No more mud holes for you.

Finding the Fabulous

Being a princess isn't all glam. There are dragons to slay along your way (rhyme unintentional!).

Looking Ahead

This week will require an honest evaluation of what holds us back. Ask God to show you the reality of why you are not moving ahead or what might be an obstacle to the life he has for you.

✦ ✦ ✦ ✦ ✦ ✦ ✦ ✦ ✦ ✦ ✦

DAY ONE: Surprise Opposition

What was your reaction when you realized you would have opposition to being a princess and to living the fabulous life from God?

As you start to make changes in your life, what reactions have you noticed from family and friends?

What are your thoughts about their responses?

I was shocked and in disbelief when everyone didn't embrace what I knew to be the fabulous princess God was shaping me into or the exciting life he had for me. Why wasn't everyone else excited with me? When we change, we shake up those around us. Describe your "cozy hut" and other hut dwellers in the "village" where you live. Does anyone there rely too much on you for self-worth or daily strength? Who?

If friends or family bristle or oppose you, it is because you are pulling the threads that interwove your lives. These are not healthy threads of love, friendship, and family but the unhealthy threads of codependency. One of the characteristics of codependency is "an unhealthy dependence on relationships. The co-dependent will do anything to hold on to a relationship; to avoid the feeling of abandonment."[62]

In a codependent relationship the other person takes the place of God in our lives, or vice versa. Yes, God made us for relationship with other people, but not to depend on them for our worth and being.

Read Matthew 22:37, 38. What does this mean to you? What does or what would it look like in your life?

Read Joshua 22:1-5. After the Israelites had settled in the promised land, three of the tribes that had been given land east of the Jordan River returned to their homes there.

As he sent them on their way, Joshua reminded them of God's instructions through Moses. Describe in your own words what each means to you:

"Love the LORD your God."

"Walk in all his ways."

"Obey his commands."

"Hold fast to him."

"Serve him with all your heart and all your soul."

One More Thing

> If you have an inkling that you might be codependent or that your family is not healthy emotionally or relationally, please consider speaking to a Christian counselor or mental health professional.[63]

Remember that you are not responsible for your friends' and family's reaction to your obedience and loving response to God, your Father. Jesus loved his family, friends, and all people, but he didn't let their opinions of him or their ideas about the way he did ministry affect God's plan for him.

If you have experienced opposition from friends and family, write the initials of those people here: _____.

Do you recall the definition of *agape love*? Write it in your own words here.

How can you show grace and agape love to friends and family who are opposing you?

Showing grace and love to those close to us who oppose us can be difficult, especially if this is new to you. If you are doing this study in a group, share ideas to help and encourage each other. Perhaps before your group meeting, the leader can contact a professional for additional ideas. Note here anything else you learn.

We all need friends to stand with us. Jesus took Peter, James, and John with him to the Garden of Gethsemane when he prayed about his impending crucifixion. In his letters Paul spoke of having one or two friends at a time stand with him in his ministry and persecutions (Romans 16:3; Philippians 2:25; 2 Timothy 1:16-18; 4:11). If God has brought you a friend or two who encourage you and support you, list them here.

If not, commit to praying about finding these people. I call them kindred spirits. My kindred spirits and I are walking with the Lord, growing in him, and not intimidated by or jealous of what God is doing in the others' lives. We pray for each other, encourage each other, and challenge each other. These relationships are not to take the place of God. As I have discussed earlier, a pulling away from others and drawing closer to God comes with the territory of living as a strong, confident princess.

Jesus too was called away to meet with God. Read Matthew 14. How many times in that chapter did Jesus get away from everyone? What was the circumstance for his need to get away (vv. 10-13)?

What circumstance interrupted his solitary time (vv. 13, 14)?

When did he finally have his time away (vv. 20-23)?

Jesus was the most in-demand person ever, yet he knew when God was calling him to solitary time, time with the Father. How do you feel about the prospect of being called apart by God, of needing people less and depending on God more?

The strong, confident princess stands firm in her relationship with her Father, the King.

✦ ✦ ✦ ✦ ✦ ✦ ✦ ✦ ✦ ✦ ✦

DAY TWO: Who's in the Mirror?

I remember being adventurous as a child and teenager. I climbed the ladder to the high dive with a bit of fear, but I wasn't going to be chicken in front of my friends. I walked to the end of the board and looked down. I thought, *Here goes*, and jumped. I rode the roller coaster time after time. Each time I felt a tinge of fear in the pit of my stomach as I approached the pinnacle of the first plunging drop, and I screamed like none other.

What happened between my teen years and adulthood? I tell my girls it was pregnancy and motherhood. In the span of a decade between the first pregnancy and birth of the last child, I lost my courage. Actually, I gained something—self-awareness. Not the healthy, normal self-awareness, but an awareness that looks back at me and says,

What are you thinking? Peter found himself in such a place after his faith-filled, adventurous self started walking on the water toward Jesus.

Turn to Matthew 14:25-33. I can just imagine Peter on the diving board at my local public pool. He would have *dived* off. In this passage Peter had been with Jesus almost three years. He'd seen some pretty amazing stuff. His faith got the better of his "common sense," and he was ready to jump out of the boat and head for Jesus. Describe a time when your adventurous faith caused you to jump right out and head for Jesus.

Look at verse 29. Jesus responded to Peter with, "Come." Can't you just see the big smile on Jesus' face? Peter, as one of Jesus' closest buds, was finally starting to get it. Maybe you haven't ever had that kind of faith. Is this study stirring that kind of faith in you? Do you sense Jesus telling you to come—to get out of the safety of your boat and "walk on water"? Describe what Jesus is calling you to do.

Read verse 30. Peter began to act like the postmaternity me—too cautious and asking himself, *What did I get myself into?* He was out there on faith, but he remembered who he was, and down he went. He was his own worst enemy. We can be our own enemy—the dragon looking back at us in the mirror. Today we will talk about three of the five fireballs we use to sabotage ourselves.

Identify an area of your life in which you struggle with perfectionism.

What has God shown you to be the motive for your perfectionism?

Review your Royal Truths. God is crazy about you and always will be.

You will mess up. You will make mistakes. You will fail. We have studied Peter a lot. Have you noticed a couple of things Peter was sure to do? One is that he made mistakes—and not just oh-I-went-to-the-wrong-address mistakes. No, I'm talking big-so-everyone-sees-and-knows-about-it mistakes. The second thing Peter was sure to do was to keep following Christ. He did not quit. God put Peter's story in the Bible not so we can say, "Glad that's not me!" He put Peter's story in the Bible so we can see a real person living out his Christian walk—warts and all—and be encouraged.

 ## One More Thing

What is the truth that will extinguish the fireball of perfectionism in your life? This is a great opportunity to graciously encourage each other if you are doing this study with a group.

The next fireball is procrastination. Procrastination is the first one to volunteer but seldom gets the job done. How have you been alerted to procrastination in your life?

What is the cause of your procrastination?

In my kitchen is a small area on the counter that I use as my headquarters. I keep my planner there, papers to be dealt with or filed, pens, tape, etc. When I procrastinate, this area quickly becomes a mess. Then three things happen: I become discouraged by the mess; I procrastinate dealing with it even more; and it takes longer to do the original tasks, because now I must make sense of the mess before I begin. Procrastination not only slows down my progress, it creates more issues for me to deal with!

Commit to a plan to address whatever is your main area of procrastination. Write it and date it.

If this seems overwhelming (and many times it is, and that's why we procrastinate), ask for help. Everyone's brain works differently. For some people organization is like breathing, but not for me. For months I prayed for help to do my ministry administrative work. Finally, I sensed God saying, "Put it out there." I did, and a dear friend volunteered. The first thing she did was to look at my files and say, "I will type all new labels." I didn't understand why my handwritten labels needed to be typed. But when she replaced my handwritten labels with her typed labels, I saw the difference. My friend is getting me organized, and she is not frustrated with the work like I am. If you need help, ask. God will provide what you need.

Identify how your procrastination is keeping you from God's plan. If you don't know, ask your husband or a close, trusted friend.

Let's end today by briefly talking about laziness. I know it seems I'm picking on you, but these issues, which seem small, will keep you from the fabulous life God has for you. I have seen it many times. It breaks my heart and fuels my passion to help you see the truth.

Someone who is lazy is "disinclined to activity or exertion : not energetic or vigorous."[64] Laziness can become a way of life. When given a choice to be productive or goof off, laziness chooses to goof off. I'm not talking about taking a well-deserved day off or spending the afternoon shopping with friends or daughters (my favorite). The book of

Proverbs is full of verses on laziness. Read Proverbs 6:6, 9; 10:4, 26; 13:4. What overall attitude regarding laziness do these verses express?

Is that the way some might describe you? Is that the way you want to be described?

The best way to combat this sly, powerful fireball is to understand the damage it causes. Think about what laziness steals from your life, from your walk with God, from the plan he has for you. List a few of these thoughts.

Think About It

One thing that fires me up to do the right thing is to realize that the enemy is getting his way when I *don't* do it. Has the enemy lulled you into a passive attitude that's making you impotent in the kingdom? Confess it to God here, ask for his help, and then accept that help.

The strong, confident princess realizes and overcomes the obstacles she has allowed into her life.

✦ ✦ ✦ ✦ ✦ ✦ ✦ ✦ ✦ ✦ ✦

DAY THREE: More Fireballs from the Dragon in the Mirror

I am not a detail person, not a *real* detail person. I work hard on whatever I'm doing, but it must have a meaningful purpose. So scrapbooking is torture for me (a minor overstatement). All that planning, cutting, taping, and placing everything just so!

Ugh! It drives me nuts. I know, I know—saving my memories forever. But for me an acid-free pretty box is good enough. (Scrapbookers, please don't e-mail me. I admire your hard work and creativity!)

We all have areas in life where we say "good enough." We accomplished the purpose or met the need. We don't need to go crazy. However, the next fireball coming our way—accepting the status quo—is loaded with that good-enough thinking about our princess lives. We tend to think like this:

+ *I'm not doing the big three—drugs, alcohol, illicit sex.*
+ *I give to the church.*
+ *I serve on the PTA.*
+ *I drive the speed limit—most of the time.*
+ *Therefore . . . I'm good enough.*

The church in Laodicea had much the same attitude. Jesus had strong words for them. Read Revelation 3:14-19. What was their offense (vv. 15, 16)?

What do they say about themselves (v. 17)?

Who in modern society do they sound like?

What does Jesus say is the truth about them (v. 17)?

What does Jesus want to do for them and why (vv. 18, 19)?

Jesus was saying, "You are missing it all! You think your wealth is it. It's not! I am It! I am ready to give you riches, righteousness, forgiveness, and vision to see the truth, but you must accept it. I am doing this all because I love you." This is the theme of *Princess Unaware*. This is my deepest desire for you and the reason for writing this book. If you miss this, you miss it all. Our fat and sassy culture is stealing the real richness of life from us. Our culture has infected us with "affluenza," and we are not even lifting our heads to look for a remedy. Life is easy. Our consciences stay moderately clear. Our lives are good, or at least good enough.

Identify how a good-enough attitude has become an obstacle to your living as the strong, confident princess.

We have one more fireball to put out today: our excuses. Don't we all have specialized ones for differing needs? We keep a few excuses handy in the kitchen drawer so that when the phone rings we are ready for whatever situation is on the other end. Our spiritual excuses are tucked in our Bibles to use when God starts to nudge us out of our comfy chairs. We pull out the excuses full of hot air when we know we should be there for our kids but would rather not be. We call in to work with our white-lie excuses.

We think these excuses are helping us, but they are keeping us from the rich life God has for us. I am inspired by author Beatrix Potter. She was in her mid-thirties when *The Tale of Peter Rabbit* was officially published, and she didn't marry until her late forties.[65] She did not let her age or the expectations of Victorian culture keep her from her passion. *Miss Potter*, the movie about her life, is on my Top Ten list. In one of my favorite scenes, Beatrix is coming home in her carriage from the meeting that resulted in her first book contract. Talking to a drawing of her fictional character Peter Rabbit, she says, "You see we cannot stay home all our lives. We must present ourselves to the world and we must look upon it as an adventure." Don't let these words of admonition be wasted on Peter Rabbit. They are powerful for us.

What excuses do you use to stay in your comfy spot?

Read Luke 9:59-62. How is Jesus calling you to follow him? Think through the areas we have discussed, plus anything else he is stirring you with. What has your answer to Jesus been?

Have you given Jesus a "yes, but" answer (v. 61)? If so, what is your excuse?

From verses 60, 62, how does Jesus answer our excuses?

Use this space to respond to Jesus regarding his words and your excuses.

We're nearing the end. Let it be the end of excuses, status quo living, laziness, procrastination, and perfectionism. Commit to God to be his strong, confident princess. Passionately seek him, know him, and pursue the plan for you that is stirring your soul.

✦ ✦ ✦ ✦ ✦ ✦ ✦ ✦ ✦ ✦ ✦

DAY FOUR: The Trickiest Dragon of All

Our final dragon to slay this week is sly, the most deceptive of all—discouragement. He often doesn't look like a dragon. In fact, we can't see him, but we hear him. He whispers his lies in our ears—lies about who we are. His whispers review our past sins and failures as evidence that we will never change, so why try? The dragon of discouragement knows which of our buttons to push to shut us down immediately.

As I collected from Christian women some of the lies and accusations the enemy uses on us, I was shocked at the struggle every woman shared. Another of the enemy's lies is to get each woman to believe that she is the only one who struggles, the only one with failures and a past. I want to share these women's discouragements with you. Be encouraged that you are not alone!

✦ When I do not have it together enough . . . when I am not being good enough . . . somehow I feel I have failed once again and God will therefore not want to hear my prayers until I clean up my act!

✦ *Who do you think you are? You are just the same small person you always were, an imposter.* I've been getting this a lot lately as I prepare [to fulfill my God-given passion]. He tries to tell me that I'm not really [my new title], that I'm just some old woman who won't be able to do what I need to do when the time comes.

✦ *You're not a very good mother. You're selfish and thoughtless. Your husband thinks you're weird, and he wonders what he got himself into. You're nothing like his mother—she's perfect.*

✦ *The heavy load of guilt and shame you carry on your shoulders for a sin committed long ago will never leave because you're not really forgiven. No Christian would ever do anything like that.*

✦ *People can see right through your facade. You're a fake. They'll hate you for it.*

✦ *You are no good at anything. You are a bad mom and wife. When people find out who you really are, they will hate you. No one likes you. You are the only one who can't keep it together.*

✦ *How can you possibly do that for God? You are so unorganized and inefficient.*

Typing those discouragements hurt me. I ache because women believe the lies! My hurt goes deeper when I imagine the hurt women have endured because of these lies, and not just once but throughout years, even decades.

What lies, accusations, or anything else does the enemy whisper in your ear to discourage you and take you out? How has the enemy challenged you with, *Did God really say . . . ?* Write these here and in your Royal Truths.

Look over your list. See these for the lies they are. Go to your Bible, your Royal Truths, and your index cards. Find what God *really* has said—a corresponding truth to slay each lie or accusation. Then write in your own words (here and in the Royal Truths) how that truth counters the enemy's lie. Here is an example:

✦ The lie: *Who do you think you are? You are just the same small person you always were, an imposter.*

✦ What God really has said: "If anyone is in Christ, he is a new creation; the old has gone, the new has come!" (2 Corinthians 5:17).

✦ Therefore: I know I am a new person, no longer what I was but now living the new life from Christ.

Some lies—*You're a bad mom; Nobody likes you; You're selfish*—remind me of a junior high bully, full of negative generalizations. Don't try to counter these lies with evidence to the contrary. That turns into a mud-slinging fight. Use the truth God has said about you. That will take the huff and puff out of the bully. Now it's your turn.

To be strong, confident princesses, we must learn to discern our Father's voice over the enemy's voice. "My sheep listen to my voice; I know them, and they follow me. I give them eternal life, and they will never perish. No one can snatch them away from me" (John 10:27, 28, *NLT*). The next time you start to feel beat down or discouraged, how will you discern where the thoughts are coming from—God's voice or Satan's demoralization?

We just need to think and ask, *Is this God's voice? What he would say to me?*

Let's close this week with truths women shared with me regarding fighting discouragement.

- ✦ Be assured that when the father of all lies is whispering discouragement, God is shouting possibility! Be strong! Preaching the Word is not for sissies!
- ✦ His throne is always approachable. He is always present and always ready and waiting to hear from me!
- ✦ Writing out the lies and accusations I hear makes me realize that these truly come from Satan, the father of lies.
- ✦ I would be happy to share the lie because by exposing it, Satan's hold will diminish!

Looking Back

How did the week go? Was it hard? eye-opening? What obstacle is the biggest hindrance to your new life as a princess? What is your plan to get it out of your way?

One more dragon to go!

chapter ten

Brave Princess

The Princess Lives with Confidence in Her Father

Princess Jessica dug her heel into her horse's side as she raced toward the drawbridge of the castle, pursued by the biggest dragon she had ever seen. The creature was black as a moonless night, with scales that shimmered red, eyes ablaze. Low to the ground the Scaly Red flew, breathing fireballs in her direction. The King had received word that Jessica was under attack, and he hurried out to receive her. His eyes locked on his daughter as she rode into the courtyard. The drawbridge closed behind her. She dismounted her horse, and the chill that had owned her heart vanished the moment she fell into her Father's strong arms.

"You are safe," the King said, "but this dragon is not yet slain." He led Jessica and the other knights onto the castle walls.

She hesitated. "Father, are you sure I'm ready for this? I've not trained long."

"This is what you were made for," he said with confidence.

The Scaly Red made a pass over the courtyard, his hot breath scorching the kingdom banners.

"Knights, ready your flaming arrows!" Jessica barked assuredly. "Fire!"

The dragon's scaly ears perked. His eyes flashed. He pitched his wings, then plummeted and landed, pinning Princess Jessica against the castle wall. His eyes were deep red pools of cunning and malice. Jessica felt his hot breath. . . .

Have you been trapped by fear as Princess Jessica was trapped by the Scaly Red? I have. For me it is a paralyzing, suffocating feeling. I feel like I can't make a decision or do the next thing. We have two options when fear pins us to the wall: we can give up, or we can fight it.

Since you have come this far in your princess adventure, I'm sure you don't want to give up. Right? Maybe the old you would have given up, but not anymore. What you need to know now is how to fight the dragon of fear.

Like the discouragement dragon, the dragon of fear is an effective warrior for the enemy. He knows what our fears are and how to best use that information against us. Likewise, our Father, the King, also knows our fears—but he knows the truth that will kill these fears in us!

Many times throughout the Bible, God tells his people, "Do not fear." In the story of Jesus' birth, God gave these words of comfort three times. First, the angel Gabriel came to Mary to give her the amazing news that she would be the mother of the Messiah. Gabriel told her, "Do not be afraid, Mary, you have found favor with God" (Luke 1:30). Second, an angel came to Joseph in a dream and told him, "Do not be afraid to take Mary home as your wife, because what is conceived in her is from the Holy Spirit" (Matthew 1:20). Third, as shepherds kept their usual night watch, a messenger of God appeared over their field. The angel's first words were, "Do not be afraid" (Luke 2:10).

We tend to be frightened when God includes us in his big plans. When God calls us to the rich life he has for us, we are fearful because it is bigger than we are, way out of our comfort zone. God told people in the Bible "Do not be afraid" because he wanted them to trust him. He says it to us for the same reason. When we are fearful, we are not trusting God and cannot be effective in living for him and serving him. We stand paralyzed, wringing our hands. Or maybe you are the rock-back-and-forth, plug-your-ears, hum-a-tune-to-block-out-the-world type. Either way, you are stuck.

The Princess Learns About Her Fear

Before we can deal with our fear, we need to know where the fear is coming from. I'm not talking about fear of snakes, heights, or germs; I'm talking about fears deep in us that drive our thoughts and actions, which Dr. Gary Smalley calls core fears. Think through these core fears and check the one or two that you believe you are most susceptible to. You often feel:

❑ helpless, powerless, impotent, or controlled
❑ rejected
❑ abandoned or left behind
❑ disconnected from others
❑ like a failure
❑ unloved (or unlovable)
❑ defective
❑ inadequate[66]

This fear is not from God. It is not his will for you to be negatively affected every time this fear is triggered in you.

My core fear of being disconnected manifests itself in feeling misunderstood. I need to know that we have an understanding between us. Of course, this is not possible all the time with all people. So I must trust God with whatever misunderstanding, misinterpretation, or misjudgment another person believes about me.

In chapter 9 I listed lies the enemy has used to discourage some fabulous Christian women:

✦ *You are not good at anything.*
✦ *When people find out who you really are, they will hate you.*
✦ *No one likes you.*
✦ *You're an imposter.*
✦ *You'll never grow in Christ because you're too weak.*

Notice how these lies take root in our core fears. Fear of being a failure, disconnected from others, unloved, inadequate—Satan identifies a core fear and uses it to fashion lies that effectively paralyze us or cause us to melt down.

Once fear takes root in our emotions, it feeds on itself. We mull it over and over, and it gets bigger and more ominous. Before anything even happens we are a wobbly mess of emotion, all because we did not address our fear with the Word of God.

Let's revisit the Israelites as they prepare to take the promised land. In Numbers 13 God had brought them near the promised land and instructed

Moses to send in spies to gather information needed to plan their attack. The spies came back with a fear-filled report: "We even saw giants there, the descendants of Anak. Next to them we felt like grasshoppers, and that's what they thought, too!" (Numbers 13:33, *NLT*). How did the Israelite spies know what the people in Canaan were thinking? The spies only saw the obstacles; then they let them grow and fill their minds with fear. They forgot what God told them in Exodus 23:30: "Little by little I will drive them out before you, until you have increased enough to take possession of the land." They focused on their fear, not the Word of God.

The Princess Is Discerning About Her Fears

As we learn about the deepest places our fears come from, we also can discern whether our fears are based on circumstances that are not our responsibility.

Situations We Don't Belong In

The Israelites were also focusing on a fight they would not have to fight until they were more prepared, and even then it would not be all at once. *Many times we are fearful of people or situations we don't need to face.*

Women especially tend to think we must be polite doormats. We stand paralyzed as someone continues to verbally punch us. I know. I have been the punching bag. We do not have to allow this!

We fear we will be rude if we allow our fight-or-flight instinct to kick in; so we endure, hoping the other person will run out of words quickly and end our beating. But the other person won't run out of words until the target is a bloody heap. This "conversation" helps no one. We are not helping the other person by allowing her to abuse us. We are not helping ourselves become better people by enduring the abuse.

Stop fearing these situations! Stop allowing yourself to be beat up! Gene and I tell our girls that no matter where they are or who they are with, if they feel uncomfortable (because of foul language, physical threats, illegal activity, or just a gut feeling) they can either remove themselves immediately from the situation or call us to come get them. If you are in a situation that turns into a sparring match and you're the one used for punching practice, graciously stop the conversation. If that doesn't work, leave or hang up the phone or get help. God did not create you to be abused by anyone. Too many women are hurt (or worse) because they did not trust their gut and get out immediately.

Joseph faced a sticky situation. He had started as a servant in the house of Potiphar, the captain of the guard of Pharaoh's army. Because God was with Joseph, he quickly advanced to have charge over all of Potiphar's household. Potiphar's wife noticed Joseph was a fine man and made advances toward him. When he refused, she poured on the pressure. She grabbed his cloak and said, "Come to bed with me!" (Genesis 39:12). What to do? The boss's wife wanted him to disobey God. If he refused, she could make his life miserable or end it. Joseph stuck with God. He ran!

My husband, Gene, has been known to have man-to-man talks with our daughters' boyfriends. The talks are not long, nor are they debasing to the young men. Gene wants the young men to know what is expected and who they will answer to if the expectations are not met. During one of these talks, he was giving the young man instructions for taking our daughter to a theme park about four hours away. Gene told him, "If you find yourself in a situation that you know you cannot win, take my daughter and run." What great advice! This is what Joseph did, and this is what we should do. In a situation where you will inevitably get beat up, run.

Worry About Other People's Reactions

Let's go back to Numbers 13. God told Moses, "Send some men to explore the land of Canaan, which I am giving to the Israelites" (v. 1). Their victory was guaranteed. They only needed to face their fears and trust God to keep his promise. When fear has our backs to the wall, God will give us grace, strength, discernment—everything we need. But we worry: *If I do what God tells me to do, the opposition will* (you fill in the blank).

Their reaction is not our concern, and we can't know their reaction in advance. If we assume we know it, we are taking God out of the equation. God tells us in

Isaiah 51:7, 8, "Listen to me, you who know right from wrong, you who cherish my law in your hearts. Do not be afraid of people's scorn, nor fear their insults. For the moth will devour them as it devours clothing. The worm will eat at them as it eats wool. But my righteousness will last forever. My salvation will continue from generation to generation" (*NLT*). No matter the reaction of those we fear, we cannot be responsible for it. We need to keep on with God.

We also worry that we will fail, the idea won't work, the ministry will fall flat, and on and on. Again, the results are not our business. Our business is to do what God gave us to do. An author puts in weeks of work before a prospective publisher sees her proposal. All the while the doubt nags: *Will anyone like this?* Then if the proposal is accepted, fear creeps in: *Can I write a whole book?* Then after the book is finished, published, and on the bookshelves, worry comes: *Will anyone buy it?* The answers to all of these questions are none of our business. We are to do the work God gave us. He has the plan and he will work it. We go back to our truth about God: "I will never leave you nor forsake you. . . . Have I not commanded you? Be strong and courageous. Do not be terrified; do not be discouraged, for the LORD your God will be with you wherever you go" (Joshua 1:5, 9).

Please know that fear is not from God and not God's plan for you.

+ Fear keeps us awake at night.
+ Fear convinces us we can't trust God.
+ Fear separates us from God.
+ Fear says we will never complete our mission.
+ Fear becomes our idol, our nemesis, our closest companion.

The Princess Fights Her Fears with Her Father's Weapons

We have three weapons to use against the dragon of fear.

The Word of God

Our first weapon is the "sword of the Spirit, which is the word of God" (Ephesians 6:17). Using Scripture as a weapon against the dragon of fear is one reason to know God's Word. This is why you have been writing your special verses on index cards and writing truths you've learned on your Royal Truths pages. These truths keep your mind focused. A focused mind lives what it focuses on. If you focus on fear and the enemy, you will live a defeated, frustrating, guilt-ridden life. If you focus on God by knowing his Word, you will live a victorious, faith-filled, fabulous life.

Fear is Satan's tool. When we battle fear, we battle the enemy. Jesus' example is our model. One of Jesus' weapons against Satan was the Word (see Matthew 4:1-11). We too need to know and speak the holy Word of God to have victory. We must read it, recite it, meditate on it. Doing so fills our minds with truth and sends the enemy on his way. Then we must do what the Word says.

Obedience

We can also battle fear with our obedience to God. In Exodus 14 the Israelites had just left Egypt and were headed toward the promised land. Pharaoh came after them with his army, and the Israelites panicked: "It would have been better for us to serve the Egyptians than to die in the desert!" (v. 12). They were only hours out of Egypt, but fear sent them into panic, and they forgot the truth about their God. Moses spoke truth and faith to the people: "Do not be afraid. Stand firm and you will see the deliverance the LORD will bring you today. . . . The LORD will fight for you; you need only to be still" (vv. 13, 14). Israel wasn't looking to God for help. They were staring at the opposition and melting in fear when they needed to get their eyes on God and his plan. God told Moses, "Why are you crying out to me? Tell the Israelites to move on. Raise your staff and stretch out your hand over the sea to divide the water so that the Israelites can go through the sea on dry ground" (vv. 15, 16).

Moses, part that sea! Israel, get a move on! Our God has a plan for us to fight our fear, and sometimes that means we need to keep doing his will and quit looking at our fears.

Another man of God on a great adventure was David. When he was still a teenage shepherd, he took on the Philistine giant, Goliath (1 Samuel 17). Goliath threw a few insults David's way, but David replied with truth, ending with, "All those gathered here will know that it is not by sword or spear that the LORD saves; for the battle is the LORD's, and he will give all of you into our hands" (v. 47). We know the outcome of the fight—David slung a stone into the forehead of Goliath and killed him.

In both of these situations, people had to trust God and then do the next thing God told them to do. Raise my staff and stretch my hand over the sea? Throw a stone at a giant who has a sword and shield? It sounds crazy to the unbelieving person—to the princess unaware. But to the woman who knows she is a princess, it is her Father's words of comfort. By his instructions God is telling us, "I've got you covered. I'm sending you into battle. Just do what I say, and I'll take care of the rest."

Confidence in God

The third weapon we need in our battle against fear is confidence in our Father. Knowing God, really knowing God, gives us the confidence we need to face our fear and fight our battles.

Long ago three men's lives depended on their confidence in God, the true King. We find them in a precarious predicament. King Nebuchadnezzar had built a golden statue ninety feet tall. The Bible does not describe the image; however, King Neb wanted all the important people in Babylon to bow to it and worship it. Whoever refused to bow would be thrown into a blazing furnace. The three young men, Shadrach, Meshach, and Abednego, would not worship anything or anyone other than God. King Neb had the young men brought to him, and he repeated his order and the consequence of not obeying. The response of these three young men reveals their confidence in God: "O Nebuchadnezzar, we do not need to defend ourselves before you in this matter. If we are thrown into the blazing furnace, the God we serve is able to save us from it, and he will rescue us from your hand, O king. But even if he does not, we want you to know, O king, that we will not serve your gods or worship the image of gold you have set up" (Daniel 3:16-18).

These three knew their God. They knew he could rescue them. They also had total confidence in God's sovereignty—even if their bodies died in the fire, their souls would instantly and forever be with God.

We too can have confidence in God because he is with us always and will give us the grace and strength to do what we need to do when we need it. "The Spirit who lives in you is greater than the spirit who lives in the world" (1 John 4:4, *NLT*). We have the victory already, but we must fight for it.

Theologian Paul Tillich has said, "Fear is the absence of faith."[67] Hebrews 11:6 says, "Without faith it is impossible to please God." God's plan for us does not include fear. It is a fabulous life lived by faith in him. God has amply equipped us to battle fear. Don't doubt that for a moment. God will never send you where he has not prepared you to go. "May the God of peace, . . . that great Shepherd of the sheep, equip you with everything good for doing his will" (Hebrews 13:20, 21). You are the strong, confident princess. Learn your battle tactics and use them with confidence in the King, your Father.

The Princess Receives a New Name

Throughout this book you and I have been on an exciting and sometimes difficult journey to the fabulous. I know it's been a lot of work. I tell my girls regarding all things meaningful and hard, "If it were easy, everyone would be doing it." This rich, abundant life is meant for everyone, but sadly, only a few pursue it. I am thrilled that you are pursuing it!

You have worked hard learning about your Father and really knowing him, knowing the truth about who you are, and letting the King show you the purpose and life he has for you. Keep adding to your Royal Truths as you advance in your princess training. Keeping truth and God's Word in your mind is one of your most powerful tools for a fabulous life.

Also keep your relationship with God ongoing. It's not just for Sunday morning or Bible study day. He is with you always and loves your company. Be real with him. He can handle anything you are feeling or going through. Remember, Jesus lived a real life on this earth in a human body. His family was not perfect, the people he did carpentry work for weren't perfect, and those he worshiped with in the synagogue weren't either. His disciples, whom he chose, were not perfect. Jesus knows people. Take your frustrations and problems to him. He understands. Take your joys and victories too. Nobody feels your joy and elation like Jesus. I'm sure he'll call the angels in to celebrate with you too.

Princess Unaware, it's time to change your name. You are the strong, confident princess. This is a truth that no one can take away from you. Turn now to the end of the Royal Truths section and fill in your name as Princess *Aware*. Date it. This is a spiritual marker for you.

Finding the Fabulous

You made it! The last week of training. I am so pleased for you. Wear your crown well. I have been privileged to lead you on this adventure!

 ## Looking Ahead

This week allow God to show you how fear limits the life he has for you. Be open to the truth God will show you about dealing with your fear.

◆ ◆ ◆ ◆ ◆ ◆ ◆ ◆ ◆ ◆ ◆

DAY ONE: Huff and Puff

The enemy uses fear to blow our houses down. Will we let him? Even the apostle Paul had fears: "When we came into Macedonia, this body of ours had no rest, but we were harassed at every turn—conflicts on the outside, fears within" (2 Corinthians 7:5). Describe a time when you were fearful.

Think of a time God called you to do something—maybe a mission, maybe an act of obedience where you usually disobey, or maybe reaching out to someone you wouldn't normally interact with. How did you feel and how did you respond?

Read Isaiah 49:1 and 2 Corinthians 3:4, 5. What two truths in these verses can you use the next time you are called to do something you wouldn't normally do?

Once again—you are called by God! We are equipped and competent through God! It's not up to us.

Let's review how another princess of God handled a mission that held lots of uncertainty. Read Luke 1:26-38. What was Mary's initial reaction to the angel's words?

The definition for *troubled* in this verse in Greek is "disturb wholly, i.e. agitate (with alarm)."[68] Mary felt like we would in this situation—scared, upset, and uncertain. What did the angel Gabriel say next?

Do you believe God says the same words to you? Why or why not?

All through the Bible are stories of other regular people fulfilling God's fabulous life for them, and God tells them not to be afraid. Through their experiences God is telling us not to be afraid. Go to your Royal Truths and find one of the truths that says you have found favor with God. Write it here.

What did the angel tell Mary next?

Mary listened and took in all the angel told her about her mission and the plan for her life. She had one question for Gabriel. What was it?

Do you feel that way? Do you want to ask God: "How can this be, since I am . . . so unprepared, unequipped, absolutely the wrong person for the job?" Go ahead and talk to God about it here.

Gabriel's answer to Mary is encouragement for us too. He told Mary, "The Holy Spirit will come upon you, and the power of the Most High will overshadow you" (v. 35). Stay with me here. I know the conception of Jesus through the Holy Spirit was a unique, never-to-happen-again miracle. But don't lose the truth here: Mary conceived Jesus by a work of the Holy Spirit; our mission from God is put in us by the Holy Spirit, and by his power it will be completed!

What were Gabriel's last words to Mary (v. 37)?

How did Mary respond to her calling and this truth (v. 38)?

How do you respond to the calling from God and the fear and uncertainty that come with it?

Review the list of core fears in the chapter. Which core fear(s) do you most identify with? Do you have a core fear that was not on Dr. Smalley's list? Write your core fear(s) here.

Do you see a correlation between your core fear(s) and the lies the enemy most often uses on you? Explain.

Satan whispers his lies. We become fearful. We stop living our fabulous life. Game point.

In studying chapter 9, what biblical truth did you write in your Royal Truths to use to combat Satan's lies?

If you did not write one or do not know one to write, choose one now. A great way to find your way around the Bible is through a concordance (some Bibles have a small one in the back). The Web site www.BibleGateway.com is an excellent resource too. Go to "keyword search" and enter a word or phrase that addresses your fear or the lie. Choose from among the verses found. Write your verse here and then transfer it to the Royal Truths.

Finally, let's look at how easy it is to let our fears turn into an all-consuming beast. Read Numbers 13:17–14:10. What was the mission of the spies (13:17-20)?

What facts did they find (13:27-29)?

What evidence did they bring home (13:23, 27)?

How did the spies respond to the facts of the obstacles Israel would face in taking the promised land (13:31–14:4, 10)?

How did faith-filled Caleb and Joshua respond to the same obstacles (13:30; 14:6-9)?

Ten spies focused on the obstacles, and their fear grew. Joshua and Caleb focused on God's faithfulness and power. They knew God was on their side. The people of the land, even though they were bigger, did not have God on their side, so their defeat was sure. What two things did Joshua and Caleb warn Moses and Aaron against succumbing to (v. 9)?

We are rebelling against God when we don't believe he will be with us and equip us and when we choose not to move ahead. What final two challenges did Joshua and Caleb give Moses and Aaron (14:9)?

These are truths we need to cling to—God is with us and we need not fear!

DAY TWO: Withstanding the Huff and Puff

Today we will discuss dealing with our fears. First, we need to identify the fears that come because we are in situations we should not be in. Sometimes we need to get out of a situation in order to be safe, emotionally or physically. We need not fear these situations, because we should not be in these situations.

Read John 10:22-39. Who was Jesus talking with?

The Jews who gathered around Jesus were not searching for the truth. They wanted to give him a hard time. What did they ask Jesus (v. 24)?

Do you hear the sarcasm in their voices? Jesus responded with truth and grace. What a great example for us! How did the Jews respond to Jesus' answer (v. 31)?

The enemy does not like it when he sees he cannot trap us in his web. When we respond with truth and grace, we are not letting him draw us in for the kill. How did Jesus make the point that they had no evidence against him (v. 32)?

It is crucial that you get this: Jesus talked with them for as long as he knew he should. When the situation turned ugly, he got out. He did not allow the Jews to take him. In John 7:1-36 Jesus was in much the same situation. "At this they tried to seize him, but no one laid a hand on him, because his time had not yet come" (v. 30). Jesus knew his time for capture and torture *would* come, but he knew this was not it.

Jesus died so we can be fellow heirs with him, princesses of the King. No one has the right to verbally, emotionally, or physically abuse God's daughters. Describe what you will do the next time you find yourself being lured into the ring for a sparring match.

Let's also put to rest our fear of the what-ifs. Others may not be pleased that you are finding the fabulous in every day. You may be worried about their reaction. Speaking truth may not appear to be "nice," but we aren't called to keep everyone happy.

Read Deuteronomy 1:19-31. Moses is recounting the story of the spies checking out the promised land. What was Moses' instruction to the Israelites (v. 29)?

What did Moses tell the Israelites to do to build their faith in God (vv. 30, 31)?

Verses 29-31 are rich in truth and principles that we need to know and hang on to. (Hmm, maybe even put on an index card!) Moses told the Israelites not to fear the enemy, because God would fight for them. Then he reminded them how God had cared for them during their years in the wilderness. What vivid imagery did Moses use to describe this relationship?

God is taking us where he wants us to go and caring for us along the way. He gives us everything we need to be victorious. Let's begin to look at our weapons from God. One of the weapons we need is the Word of God.

Read Matthew 4:1-11. Who led Jesus to the desert, and for what purpose?

This time of temptation was God's will for his Son—a tough concept to understand. Does it stand to reason that we will go through times of testing and battle also? Explain your thoughts.

When did the temptation begin? What was Jesus' physical condition?

Note the way the devil worded his challenge to Jesus (v. 3). What did he say?

Satan challenged Jesus with a bit of truth and tried to add to it a temptation based on a lie: "If you are really God's Son, you have every right and power to turn stones to bread to take care of your legitimate hunger." How did Jesus respond (v. 4)?

If your Bible gives a cross-reference in the margin or footnote, you'll see that Jesus was quoting Deuteronomy 8:3. Look it up.

What happened next (Matthew 4:5, 6)?

Jesus was presented with another temptation. Satan used the same truth-plus-lie technique: since Jesus was God's Son, he should throw himself off the highest point of the temple and see how God would save him. But Satan added something new this time. What phrase did Satan use to show he could quote Scripture?

Satan actually *misused* Scripture, another form of lying. Look up the cross-reference for these verses (Psalm 91:11, 12). How did Jesus respond (Matthew 4:7)?

Throughout this book, I've tried to convey a basic principle of Bible study—we cannot pull verses out of their context and make them say what we want. We must make sure we understand the consistent message of the Bible. "Do your best to present yourself to God as one approved, a workman who does not need to be ashamed and who correctly handles the word of truth" (2 Timothy 2:15). *The Ryrie Study Bible* comments that correctly handling the Word means "in both analysis and presentation—in contrast to the inane interpretations of false teachers."[69] Satan gave Jesus an inane interpretation of Psalm 91:11, 12. Jesus responded in Matthew 4:7 with Scripture from Deuteronomy 6:16. Look that up and write it here.

One more time the devil tried to get Jesus (Matthew 4:8, 9). Recall a time when you were offered something magnificent.

Satan tried to tempt Jesus with a lie—showing Jesus all he could have if he bowed down. Temptation promises us the world (a world it can't deliver) but gives us spiritual death. What was Jesus' answer (v. 10)?

Jesus was quoting Deuteronomy 6:13. Look it up.

Do you see how Jesus knew Scripture, used it appropriately, and defeated the enemy with it? Of course, we cannot just say the words and expect victory. We must mean them and position ourselves to do what they say.

✦ ✦ ✦ ✦ ✦ ✦ ✦ ✦ ✦ ✦ ✦

DAY THREE: God Handles the Huff and Puff

Today we will connect what we know about God with how to deal with fear. We will look at two other weapons God has given us—obedience and our confidence in him.

Recently my daughters acted out for me the explosion of drama that takes place every time two of the girls they know get together. For those of you who haven't been around teen girls for a while, the tone of the conversation is shock and from high on the speakers' self-righteous perches:

"Oh my gosh! Did you hear what Sarah said about Jenn?"
"I know! I would never!"
"I mean, really!"

Watching my daughters perform this parody makes me laugh—they're natural actresses. The sad part is, their friends are caught up in the drama as real life; they can't see past the drama to the right way to respond to the situation. In Exodus 14 we see the Israelites doing their version of teen drama. Read verses 10-12 in teen drama voice:

"Land o' Goshen! We are doing to die!"
"I know! God won't take care of us!"
"I mean, we told Moses to leave us in Egypt, and now look at the mess we're in!"
"I would never have left if I'd known I was going to die in the desert!"
"I mean, really!"

Do you ever immerse yourself in drama when the enemy is after you? Explain.

It does seem easier to do drama than to obey. How did Moses calm the nearly hysterical Israelites (vv. 13, 14)?

How hard is it for you to be still in the midst of fear? to believe God is the one fighting for you?

After Moses calmed the Israelites, what instruction did God give them (vv. 15, 16)?

What reinforcements did God provide so the Israelites could obey him (vv. 19-22)?

God provides whatever and whomever we need in order to obey. Help comes from the Holy Spirit, angels, and in other ways—both supernatural and natural—that we do not always see. We need to show up, do what God says, and trust him with the results.

I can't think of three men whose lives depended on the character of God and who lived that reality more than Shadrach, Meshach, and Abednego. Turn to their story in Daniel 3, when an angry King Neb summoned them. Read verses 13-15. How would you feel if the source of your fear was in your face like this?

How did our guys respond? What truths about God did they state (vv. 16-18)?

First, they knew God was their defender. They did not need to defend their position. They knew God was able to save them. They knew he would rescue them from King Neb's attempts to rule them; either he would bring them out of the fire or he would take them into Heaven. Either way, King Neb couldn't hurt them. And either way, they would stay faithful to their faithful God.

Their response reflected their intimate relationship with God. They had lived in pagan Babylon since their teen years. I'm sure this was not the first time they had trusted God and defended their faith in a tight situation. We come to know God better and better the longer we walk with him. We will talk more about their results at the end of today's study.

One more reason we have confidence in God in the face of our fears is the grace and strength he gives us when we need it. I have friends who have faced hard times—the death of a spouse, the death of a child, terminal disease . . . I am amazed at their strength and grace.

My dear friend Katherine went through years of slowly losing her young husband to cancer. She took on all the responsibilities for the family, yet she never felt sorry for herself. She was the first to think of others. I asked her how she did it. She told me, "A strong, unmovable faith that God loves me, knows, and only does what is best for me and my family. And that he has a wonderful plan and purpose in motion in and through it all (the mess and madness), even though I may never truly find out all the good he had going on!" She continued, "I am at peace with believing in God without having to have all the answers! He has the answers, and somehow that is good enough for me! He placed that satisfaction in me! I was backed in the corner, and my heart yearned to gain his perspective."

The same grace and strength is available to us as we face the fearful times in our lives. But we must choose it. Read Isaiah 40:28-31. How does this passage speak to your fearful spirit?

Maybe your situation, like Katherine's, has been going on for a long time. How does your choice to trust God and "gain his perspective," combined with the power of this Scripture, renew you?

Will you now place yourself in a posture to trust God and gain his perspective the next time you are face-to-face with a fearful situation—whether it be confrontation, crisis, or an out-of-the-box opportunity? Talk to God and commit to it here.

Think About It

You have just entrusted your life to the God who loves you like crazy and created the universe. You will find no safer place.

Let's finish today with another quick visit with our guys in Babylon—Shadrach, Meshach, and Abednego. When we left them, they were just about to feel the wrath of King Neb. Turn back to Daniel 3:16-30. How did the three respond to the king (vv. 17, 18)?

Isn't their boldness amazing! Read verse 28. Can the same be said about you—that you trust, worship, and serve God only, defying the world's negative pressure to conform and willing to give your life rather than conform? Will you commit to God that you will live for him and serve him, no matter the risk or the outcome?

✦ ✦ ✦ ✦ ✦ ✦ ✦ ✦ ✦ ✦ ✦

DAY FOUR: You Made It!

Princess Aware, you made it! This is the last day of our journey together. What a trip! Your fabulous life is waiting for you to live each day. You do that by remembering, believing, and living the truths you learned.

I tell the young women I mentor, "I reserve the right to call you with one more thing after we get together." (I often think of one more thing I want to say!) Today I want to give you several "one more things" to think about—to give you the firm hug I would give you if we were face-to-face.

Read Psalm 139:1-18 whenever you start to think you are insignificant and God has forgotten you. What do verses 14, 16 say about you and your life?

You and your life are so precious to God that he planned it all even before you were born.

Read Psalm 138:8. The wording in the *New American Standard Bible* speaks to my soul: "The Lord will accomplish what concerns me; your lovingkindness, O Lord, is everlasting; do not forsake the works of Your hands." What does this verse tell you about God's involvement in your fabulous life?

What did David mean by "the works of Your hands"?

You are "the works of God's hands." And he will not forsake you. Did you write a verse about this in your Royal Truths? (I like Joshua 1:5.)

Read Deuteronomy 31:1-8. What is the occasion of Moses' speech?

What instructions did Moses give the Israelites in verses 6, 8?

What assurances did Moses give the Israelites in those same two verses to help them obey the Lord?

God is for us. He wants us to be strong and courageous in him so we can boldly live our fabulous lives. Before we leave Moses, Joshua, and the Israelites, read Joshua 11:15. That is my prayer for you—to leave nothing undone that God gives you to do.

One last visit with Gideon, our reluctant hero. The angel of God found Gideon hiding from the enemy in a winepress. Read Judges 6:11-14. What encouragement did the angel give Gideon (v. 12)?

After all we have studied, do you believe this about yourself, mighty princess?

How does this truth change the way you will live your life? I know it is all-encompassing, so explain your attitude shift and a few nuts-and-bolts details.

Describe a time you felt as Gideon did in verse 13.

What was God's response to Gideon in verse 14?

This is what we have been talking about—going out with what God has given you. God will give you what you need as you need it, but you must act on what you know and what he is telling you to do. Hear God's words to you: "Am I not sending you?" God is sending you to a fabulous life of adventure with him. Yes, some days you will say with Gideon, "If the LORD is with us, why has all this happened?" But you know deep in your heart that God is with you—and it's in your Royals Truths to remind you!

I want to leave you with this prayer from Colossians 1:10-12, as my prayer for you. I pray that you will do each of these things:

- ✦ Live a life worthy of the Lord.
- ✦ Please him in every way.
- ✦ Bear fruit in every good work.
- ✦ Grow in the knowledge of God.
- ✦ Be strengthened with all power according to his glorious might.
- ✦ Have great endurance and patience.
- ✦ Joyfully give thanks to the Father.

God "has qualified you to share in the inheritance of the saints in the kingdom of light" (v. 12). He "rescued us from the dominion of darkness and brought us into the kingdom of the Son he loves" (v. 13). You are redeemed and forgiven. You are rescued from darkness and now live in the kingdom of the Son. You are Princess Aware!

We end our journey together with the climax of the story of Princess Jessica. I dedicate it to you.

✦　✦　✦　✦　✦　✦　✦　✦　✦　✦　✦

"Jessica! The sword of truth!" cried her Father. "Here!"
A sword with a long, flashing blade came flying through the air in her direction.
The sword!

She reached out, caught the sword, and plunged it into the beast's heart. She slid from his grasp. He fell limp. Once more, she ran into her Father's arms. . . .

Once again it was time to leave the safety of the castle and fulfill the King's purpose for her. Once again she had her satchel with provisions and the precious book tucked inside. She walked beside the King, leading one of his own strong steeds, for she was not the young woman who had come strolling into the castle sometime before, wearing gingham and thinking fairy-tale thoughts.

"How long, Father?" she dared to ask.

He said somberly, "Your service in my kingdom will never end, Jessica." Then he brightened. "Neither will my love for you. I love you all so deeply."

"I know," said Jessica. "You even love Sarah."

"Of course Sarah! With my whole heart! You all have lessons to learn, and I am patient."

They stopped at the drawbridge. The King said, "Princess, you will always have provisions. There are other knights stationed along the way to assist you. And falcons keep watch from the skies."

Jessica mounted the horse and raised her sword, her heart bursting with love and pride. "May the King live forever! And may his kingdom dwell in peace."

The King nodded agreement. "It has been written in the book, daughter, and it will be done. In my strength go. In my strength return."

"I miss you already, Father." She gazed for a moment at the castle and its friendly, bustling courtyard. "And I will miss my home."

"Another dragon is down, Jessica, but the war continues. You will find some villages in great danger, some in great need. And remember, enemies take many forms. But know this: as far as my kingdom stretches—even beyond sea and star—there you are always at home."

Princess Jessica gave the horse a quick swat, and off she went across the drawbridge. Through the meadow she sped, whispering to herself as a brisk wind chilled her face, "Your kingdom, my home . . . Your kingdom, my home . . ."

Royal Truths

A Section to Personalize

Royal truths about the King, my heavenly Father, God:

_____

_____

_____

_____

_____

_____

_____

_____

_____

_____

_____

Royal truths about me, a princess, child of the King:

_____

_____

_____

_____

_____

_____

_____

_____

_____

_____

_____

_____

_____

Date I became a princess of the King:

_____

How I define success:

_____

_____

_____

_____

_____

My princess priorities:

_____

_____

_____

_____

_____

What God has called me to do:

_____

_____

_____

_____

_____

_____

My Principle of Neglect plan:

_____

_____

_____

_____

_____

_____

_____

Lie(s) the enemy most often uses on me:

_____

_____

_____

_____

_____

_____

_____

_____

_____

_____

_____

_____

_____

The specific truth from the Bible that fights Satan's lies about me:

_____

_____

_____

_____

_____

_____

_____

_____

_____

_____

_____

_____

_____

The truth about these lies is that they are not true about me! The truth is:

_____

_____

_____

_____

_____

_____

_____

_____

_____

_____

_____

✦ ✦ ✦ ✦ ✦ ✦ ✦ ✦ ✦ ✦ ✦

I, _____ , am the strong, confident princess,

Princess Aware!

Date: _____

Notes

1. James Strong, *Strong's Exhaustive Concordance of the Bible* (Chattanooga, TN: AMG), 76, Greek Dictionary of the New Testament.

2. Ibid., 45, 106.

3. Ibid., 96.

4. Ibid., 59.

5. Ibid., 6.

6. Ibid., 28.

7. Joseph M. Stowell, *Simply Jesus: Experiencing the One Your Heart Longs For* (Sisters, OR: Multnomah, 2002), 51.

8. *Pride and Prejudice* (2005), http://www.imdb.com/title/tt0414387/quotes (accessed January 5, 2009).

9. Strong, *Exhaustive Concordance*, 5.

10. http://www.merriam-webster.com/dictionary/benevolence.

11. Charles C. Ryrie, ed., *The Ryrie Study Bible, New American Standard Translation* (Chicago: Moody, 1976, 1978), 1744.

12. *Indiana Jones and the Last Crusade* (1989). Screenplay by Jeffrey Boam, www.weeklyscript.com/Indiana (accessed January 23, 2009).

13. Wayne Grudem, *Systematic Theology* (Leicester, Great Britain: Inter-Varsity Press and Grand Rapids, MI: Zondervan, 1994), 217.

14. Strong, *Exhaustive Concordance*, 118, Hebrew and Chaldee Dictionary of the Old Testament.

15. Ibid., 73.

16. Grudem, *Systematic Theology*, 315.

17. Ibid., 320.

18. Ibid., 321.

19. Strong, *Exhaustive Concordance*, 28, Hebrew and Chaldee Dictionary of the Old Testament.

20. Beth Moore, *Daniel: Lives of Integrity, Words of Prophecy* (Nashville, TN: LifeWay Press, 2006), 53.

21. Strong, *Exhaustive Concordance*, 11, Greek Dictionary of the New Testament.

22. http://www.biblegateway.com/resources/dictionaries/dict_meaning.php?source=1&wid=T0002926&interface=print (accessed January 5, 2009).

23. Strong, *Exhaustive Concordance*, 57, Greek Dictionary of the New Testament.

24. Strong, *Exhaustive Concordance*, 156, Hebrew and Chaldee Dictionary of the Old Testament.

25. Oswald Chambers, *My Utmost for His Highest: Selections for the Year* (Uhrichsville, OH: Barbour, copyright renewed 1963), 174.

26. If you want to study more on personality types, I recommend the following classic books: *Spirit-Controlled Temperament* by Tim LaHaye, *Personality Plus* by Florence Littauer, and *The Treasure Tree* by Gary Smalley and John Trent. And if you'd like to have some real fun analyzing six different personality types categorized according to characters in the Winnie the Pooh books, check out *Personalities According to Pooh* by Elizabeth Baker (releasing July 1, 2009, Standard Publishing).

27. Beth Moore, *Loving Well Journal* (Nashville, TN: LifeWay Press, 2007), 56.

28. Chambers, *My Utmost*, 174.

29. Ryrie, *Study Bible*, 1862.

30. Strong, *Exhaustive Concordance*, 82, Greek Dictionary of the New Testament.

31. Personal testimony shared with the author. Used by permission.

32. Joseph M. Stowell, *Following Christ: Experiencing Life the Way It Was Meant to Be* (Grand Rapids, MI: Zondervan, 1996), 193.

33. Strong, *Exhaustive Concordance*, 5, Greek Dictionary of the New Testament.

34. Ibid., 20.

35. Grudem, *Systematic Theology*, 386.

36. http://www.merriam-webster.com/dictionary/trust.

37. Ryrie, *Study Bible*, 1454.

38. Strong, *Exhaustive Concordance*, 78, 104, Greek Dictionary of the New Testament.

39. Grudem, *Systematic Theology*, 1016.

40. *Discover Your Spiritual Gifts the Network Way* by Bruce Bugbee (Zondervan) and *Maximizing Your Effectiveness* by Aubrey Malphurs (Baker) are excellent books I recommend to help you discover and understand your spiritual gifts.

41. These definitions taken from Aubrey Malphurs, *Maximizing Your Effectiveness: How to Discover and Develop Your Divine Design* (Grand Rapids, MI: Baker, 1995), 50–55.

42. Check out various Bible study resources at www.standardpub.com. Two parachurch organizations, Community Bible Study (http://www.communitybiblestudy.org/) and Bible Study Fellowship (http://www.bsfinternational.org/), offer groups throughout the United States and internationally (Web sites accessed January 5, 2009).

43. Jessica Mador, "Hundreds gather at the 35W bridge to remember," August 1, 2008, http:// minnesota.publicradio.org/display/web/2008/08/01/memorial_service/ (accessed January 5, 2009).

44. Sea Stachura, "NTSB closer to answering why the bridge went down," August 1, 2008, http://minnesota.publicradio.org/display/web/2008/07/31/ bridgeinvestigation_update (accessed January 5, 2009).

45. Calvin Miller, *The Power of Living for God's Pleasure* (Wheaton, IL: Tyndale, 2003), 57.

46. Chambers, *My Utmost*, 14.

47. *Chariots of Fire* (1981), http://www.imdb.com/title/tt0082158/quotes.

48. Miller, *Power of Living*, 57.

49. Ibid.

50. *Maximizing Your Effectiveness: How to Discover and Develop Your Divine Design* by Aubrey Malphurs (Baker) and *Discover Your Spiritual Gifts the Network Way* by Bruce L. Bugbee (Zondervan) both include a spiritual gifts assessment test.

51. Strong, *Exhaustive Concordance*, 96, Greek Dictionary of the New Testament.

52. Chambers, *My Utmost*, 142.

53. I recommend the following books to help you get your look put together: *Reinvent Yourself with Color Me Beautiful: Four Seasons of Color, Makeup, and Style* by JoAnne Richmond (Taylor Trade); *Dress Your Best: The Complete Guide to Finding the Style That's Right for Your Body* by Clinton Kelly and Stacy London (Three Rivers); *How Not to Look Old: Fast and Effortless Ways to Look 10 Years Younger, 10 Pounds Lighter, 10 Times Better* by Charla Krupp (Springboard); *Style 101: What Every Stylish Woman Should Know* by the editors of *In Style* magazine.

54. Chambers, *My Utmost*, 71.

55. Ibid., 364.

56. Phil Vischer, *Me, Myself, & Bob* (Nashville, TN: Thomas Nelson, W Publishing Group, 2006), 219.

57. Strong, *Exhaustive Concordance*, 161, Hebrew and Chaldee Dictionary of the Old Testament.

58. Ibid., 108.

59. Matthew Henry, *Matthew Henry's Commentary on the Whole Bible* (Peabody, MA: Hendrickson, 1991), 1676.

60. Michael Kranish, "Palin's daughter, 17, is pregnant," September 2, 2008, http://www.boston.com/news/nation/articles/2008/09/02/palins_daughter_17_is_pregnant?/ (accessed January 5, 2009).

61. http://www.asas.asicseurope.com/A-ZONE/News.htm?contentid=313 (accessed January 5, 2009).

62. http://www.nmha.org/go/codependency (accessed January 5, 2009). Visit this site for more information on codependency and dysfunctional families.

63. You may also want to check out this Web site: http://www.nmha.org/go/codependency (accessed February 25, 2009).

64. http://www.merriam-webster.com/dictionary/lazy.

65. Information in this section was taken from http://www.peterrabbit.com.

66. http://www.smalleyonline.com/articles/truth/corefear.html (accessed January 5, 2009).

67. Paul Tillich, http://www.cybernation.com/quotationcenter/quoteshow.php?type=author&id=8951 (accessed January 5, 2009).

68. Strong, *Exhaustive Concordance*, 28, Greek Dictionary of the New Testament.

69. Ryrie, *Study Bible*, 1826.